Better
English
Usage

WEBSTER'S WORD POWER

Better English Usage

BETTY KIRKPATRICK

GEDDES & GROSSET

WEBSTER'S **WORD POWER**

Betty Kirkpatrick, a graduate of Edinburgh University, has a long career in reference publishing. She has edited *Chambers Twentieth Century Dictionary, Roget's Thesaurus*, the concise edition of *Brewer's Phrase and Fable*, and was language consultant to the *Encarta World English Dictionary*. She has compiled various other reference books, including the *Oxford Paperback Thesaurus* and the *Bloomsbury Dictionary of Clichés*. She acts as a consultant to the *Bloomsbury Good Word Guide*. Betty is author of an extensive list of publications on various aspects of the English language for learners of English.

Published 2021 by Geddes & Grosset, an imprint of
The Gresham Publishing Company Ltd.,
31, Six Harmony Row, Glasgow,
G51 3BA, Scotland, UK

ISBN 978-1-84205-760-5

This book is not published by the original publishers of
Webster's Dictionary or by their successors.

BETTER ENGLISH USAGE

Better English Usage is an introduction to modern English usage using memorable examples of common errors and misconceptions, as well as examples of good usage. Errors can be made even by fluent English speakers. Learn how to avoid them with this simple guide written in a friendly, accessible style.

Gain a better understanding of how the English language works as we discuss how usage changes and evolves over time. This guide explains why certain mistakes might be made, with the thinking that an understanding of the issue might enable readers to remember the correct usage more easily. We talk about the rules of grammar, but also about when it is acceptable, and even necessary, to break those rules.

This is an engaging and accessible volume to improve your understanding of the intricacies of English usage. It includes chapters on:

- Contemporary English usage
- Words and phrases that are easily confused
- Common errors in English
- The changing face of English

WEBSTER'S **WORD POWER**

CONTENTS

1

THE CHANGING FACE OF ENGLISH

We have witnessed the most amazing number of changes in society in recent decades. Many of them have taken place so rapidly that some of us can scarcely keep up with the speed of change.

The most obvious speedy changes have taken place in technology but technological changes have affected many other walks of life, indeed most walks of life. They have affected everything from medicine to transport to entertainment to communications. Language is not immune from these changes. At the very least, it has had to accommodate names for the many new things and processes that the technological changes have led to.

HISTORICAL CHANGES IN VOCABULARY

Language is no stranger to change. In fact it reflects everything that happens in life. If it is out there, there must be a word for it. An obvious example of how events in a particular country affect language is the effect that the various invaders of what are now the British Isles had on the English language.

For example, the Vikings may be best remembered for their plundering and pillaging but they left behind a useful linguistic heritage. Thanks to them we have words such as *law*, *skill*, *egg*, *knife*, *skate* and many more.

The Norman invasion, masterminded by William the Conqueror in 1066, gave rise to even more words entering the English language. This French influence gave us *justice*, *money*, *action* and *village*, to name but a few.

English explorers and traders also contributed to the growth of the English language by bringing back words from the various places they visited. For example, the language acquired *umbrella*, *granite* and *bandit* from Italian, *bungalow*, *cot*, *shampoo* and *chintz* from Hindi and *cigar*, *cork* and *negro* from Spanish. This last word was to cause much controversy in later times and came to be regarded as very offensive.

The Renaissance of the 16th and 17th centuries, with its revival of classical scholarship and a renewed interest in Latin and Greek, had a great effect on the English language. During this time many Latin and Greek words underwent a process of naturalization and ended up in English. A few examples include *crisis*, *vital*, *locate*, *credible*, *exclaim* and *apparatus*. This was a very busy time for the English language.

Over the centuries there have been many sources that have provided new words for the English language. From Japanese, English has acquired *judo*, *tsunami*, *karaoke* and *sushi*, from Chinese, *tea*, *ketchup* and *kowtow*, and from Yiddish, *spiel*, *kosher* and *chutzpah*. From Russian, English acquired *czar/tsar*, *glasnost*, *icon*, *perestroika* and *vodka* and Australia supplied it with *boomerang*, *budgerigar* and *kangaroo*. It seems that the English language is like a magpie, forever picking up new shiny items to add to its already rich store.

CHANGES OF MEANING

The changes in the English language are by no means restricted to vocabulary additions. Changes also occur once the words are part of the English language. Sometimes the changes involve meaning. A classic historical example of meaning change relates to the word *silly*. Now it means 'foolish, lacking sense or judgement', but this meaning only evolved gradually. The word *silly* is derived from Old English *gesaelig*, meaning 'happy'. This became first *seely* in Middle English and then *silly*. As the form of the word changed, so did its meaning. It went from meaning 'happy' to meaning 'blessed or pious'.

The change in the meaning of *silly* continued. From 'pious' the meaning became 'innocent', then 'harmless' and then 'to be pitied'. This became 'feeble' and then 'feeble in the mind'. From this it was an easy step to the modern meaning of the word. This is, of course, an example of a change that is both extreme and historical.

WORDS WHOSE MEANING HAS CHANGED

There have been many more changes in meaning throughout the centuries and they are still occurring. A few of them are listed below.

decimate

The verb **decimate** literally means to kill or destroy one in ten of a set of people. It is derived from a Latin word meaning 'to kill one in ten of a unit of soldiers who took part in a mutiny'. The practice was doubtless intended to act as a warning to the other nine units.

Nowadays there is not much call for a word meaning 'to kill one in ten people' and the word has moved on. It came to mean 'to kill a large proportion of', as in:

> *The disease decimated the rabbit population of the island.*

One tenth is not a huge proportion of a whole and so possibly there was a mix-up somewhere between one tenth being killed and one tenth surviving.

The word moved on even further and came to mean 'to inflict a great deal of damage on something or to destroy a large number or part of', as in:

> *The event attracted a lot of adverse publicity to the area and decimated the tourist industry.*

There was a great deal of opposition to the changes in meaning of **decimate**. It seems that people did not want to let go of its connection with ten. It is advisable not to mention a specific amount when you are using the word.

hopefully

Changes in the language are frequently met with great opposition, at least until people get used to them, or until the loudest of the objectors are no longer with us. The opposition to the introduction of **hopefully** was particularly forceful. I am talking, of course, about **hopefully** in the sense of 'it is to be hoped that', as

> *Hopefully, we'll get there in time for dinner.*

rather than 'with hope', as

> *We waited hopefully for their arrival until it*
> *became clear that they were not coming.*

Even now people still grumble about it, although **hopefully** in its later sense is now regarded as quite acceptable, except, perhaps, in the most formal of contexts. The arguments against the acceptance of **hopefully** in its more recent meaning were not really convincing. Much was made of the possibility of ambiguity occurring, especially when the adverb is placed immediately before the verb, as in:

> *They will hopefully wait for us although we're going*
> *to be a bit late.*

However, the **hopefully** in the sentence above is much more likely to mean 'it is to be hoped that' and, if there are genuine possibilities of ambiguity, you can change its position to the beginning of the sentence.

disinterested/uninterested

Until very recently **disinterested** meant the same as *'impartial'* or *'unbiased'*. It was often confused with **uninterested**, meaning 'not having any interest in something', and now it has come to share this meaning. This has been a gradual change and many young people are not aware that the distinction between the meanings of the two words ever existed.

This change has not been universally welcomed by any means. Many people, especially older people, still protest about it and claim that changes like this are spoiling what they see as the purity of the English language. This is often now referred to as 'a dumbing down' of the language. In fact this particular example of a language change is actually a reversion to the previous state of affairs. According to historical dictionaries from the 17th century **disinterested** could mean the same as **uninterested**.

aggravate/irritate

Aggravate is another word with a long-established meaning that has acquired another meaning. This still arouses protest from people who consider themselves language purists and guardians of the language. They consider that the only proper meaning of **aggravate** is 'to make worse', as in:

> *His headache was aggravated by the loud music*
> *playing next door.*

This meaning is admittedly the older, having come into being in the late 16th century. However, the meaning 'to irritate or annoy', as

> *Those children have been aggravating*
> *the neighbours all day with their noisy games.*

is not far behind in terms of age. It first made an appearance in the early 17th century. It is this meaning that so irritates – we had better not say aggravates – some users, often older users.

gay

Some people disliked the widespread introduction of the homosexual meaning of the English adjective **gay**. The word had been used in this meaning in a very limited way since the 1930s, but it did not reach a wider audience until the late 1960s. It was used by the gay community and the usage seems to have been driven by them. Now it has become such an established meaning of **gay** in the English-speaking world that it has edged out the original use of 'merry or light-hearted', it's rather unusual to hear it used in this sense now.

When the homosexual meaning of gay first came into widespread use, some people mourned the passing of **gay**'s original happy meaning. However, the word *homosexual* was more in need of a positive synonym than the word *merry* was. It is an example of a word being chosen to fill an obvious need. This adjective has the advantage of being neutral and nonjudgmental, and while there are quite a few synonyms for **gay** in its original sense, there are not very many for the homosexual meaning. Words such as *bent* and *queer* are intended to be offensive.

Note that the abstract noun from **gay** in its homosexual sense is **gayness**, while the abstract noun from **gay** in its merry, light-hearted sense is **gaiety**.

queer

The mention of **queer** raises an interesting aspect of language and, indeed, an interesting aspect of people. **Queer** had the original meaning of 'odd or improper'. The phrase *on queer street* meant in financial difficulties.

In the early 20th century **queer** came to be used as an informal, derogatory term for *homosexual* but it is now being reclaimed by the LGBTQIA+ (lesbian, gay, bisexual, trans, queer, intersex, asexual) community as an umbrella term that is more inclusive of the whole community.

sexy
Sexy was originally an informal word meaning 'causing, or intended to cause, desire', as in:

> *She bought a sexy new dress.*

It then went on to acquire an additional meaning that is not related to sex. This meaning is 'interesting, attractive or exciting', often because of being new or fashionable, as in:

> *We are about to launch a sexy new range of kitchen equipment.*

> *They're planning to pull down the old building and build what they call a sexy new state-of-the-art office block.*

MORE VOCABULARY CHANGES

The above are some of the best-known changes in meaning. However, other words have been affected also. Changes like the ones that follow tend to take place very gradually and it takes some time before people become aware that a change is taking place.

SLOW BUT SURE

historic/historical
It looks as though a change is affecting these two adjectives which are derived from the word *history*. The adjectives are **historic** and **historical**, and traditionally they have different meanings.

Strictly speaking, **historic** refers to an event that is important enough or memorable enough to be recorded in history, as in:

> *The Battle of Waterloo was a historic victory for the British.*

It is now often used exaggeratedly of an event, often a sporting event, that is not nearly as important as that description suggests, as in:

> *The cup final ended in a historic victory for the Spanish team.*

According to traditional usage, **historical** simply refers to something that took place in the past or means 'based on the study of history', as in:

> *Most of the country's historical records are held in the national archive.*

Probably because these words sound so alike and are so frequently confused the distinction between them is beginning to disappear. This is bound to arouse some protest. Change always does.

fortuitous/fortunate

Signs of change are particularly likely to go unspotted for a while where the word affected is not very commonly used. **Fortuitous** is such a word. Originally, and in line with its derivation, **fortuitous** meant 'happening by chance' or 'accidental', as in:

> *She bumped into her old friend in a completely fortuitous meeting. They hadn't seen each other since they were at school together.*

Because the words sound quite similar, **fortuitous** began to become confused with **fortunate**, as in:

> *Meeting her father's old friend was fortuitous for her because he offered her a job in his company.*

And in time **fortuitous** began to be used to describe an event that was not only accidental but also lucky.

nauseous

Nauseous is another word that appears to be undergoing a change, but it is not exactly a word in everyday use and the change may not yet be very obvious. The adjective **nauseous** in British English traditionally means 'nauseating' or 'causing nausea'.

In other words, it is a formal way of saying something makes you feel sick or want to vomit, as in:

> *There was a nauseous smell of rotten meat coming from the fridge.*

In American English **nauseous** means 'nauseated' or 'feeling sick' or 'about to vomit', as in:

> *Going on a boat trip always makes me feel nauseous, even when the sea is calm.*

The British English equivalent of American English **nauseous** is **nauseated**, but users of British English have begun to adopt the American usage, as in:

> *She says that she felt nauseous for most of her pregnancy.*

OTHER SIGNS OF CHANGE

There have been other signs of change. For example, the distinction between **imply** and **infer** is fading fast. Because many people do not understand the distinction between **fewer** and **less** (it should be fewer bottles but less wine) this distinction is also fading, especially in informal contexts.There is a considerable amount of protest about this. Perhaps the greatest protest of all is aimed at the fading distinction between **all right** and **alright**. For more information on these words go to Chapter 8.

CHANGES IN ACCOMPANYING VERBS

The examples that follow show a change of accompanying verb not a change of meaning.

data

Data is the plural form of the word **datum** but the singular form **datum** is rarely used now. As a plural noun, **data** was formerly always used with a plural verb, as in:

> *The data released by the bank were carefully*
> *studied by financial journalists.*

In modern usage **data** is often accompanied by a singular verb, as in:

> *The data on which the research was based has*
> *been found to be inaccurate.*

Formerly **data** was used mainly in a scientific or technical context, but it is now frequently used with reference to computer information, and so is in more general use. Data is the regular plural form of the singular Latin noun datum but, since Latin is no longer taught in many British schools, this fact is not now very well known. Many people simply did not know why **data** should be considered plural and so its singular form **datum** is fading from use.

media

Media is the plural form of **medium** when this refers to a means of transmitting information, as in:

> *Television is certainly a useful educational medium*
> *for children.*

> *The most popular forms of news media were found*
> *to be radio and television.*

The word **media** is frequently found in the expression the media, which is used to refer to the means of mass communication, i.e. newspapers, radio and television. The use of **media** as a singular noun is disliked by some people, but this use is becoming increasingly common, as in:

> *The media is often blamed for making young people*
> *body-conscious.*

Many people now do not know that media is the plural form of the Latin word medium, and see no reason why it should not be used in the singular.

THE AMERICAN INFLUENCE

Many people who feel that the English language has been dumbed down blame this on America. Some say that the Americans are to blame for the many slang words and colloquialisms that we now have. Admittedly, we do tend to borrow a lot of words from American English, and the globalization of communication has increased this trend. America is a productive and inventive country and this productivity and inventiveness have been extended to its language. To some extent British English has been affected by this.

programme/program

There is no doubt that American English is having an effect on British English usage. For example, we still stick with the British English spelling **programme** when we want to refer to something that is on TV, or to what is on offer in a concert or at the theatre. However, British English follows American English when it comes to the international world of computers and opts for **program** in that context.

disc/disk

A similar thing happened to the word **disc**. When this was applied to computers in British English it became **disk**, as in hard disk, in line with the American spelling. Other meanings retained the **disc** spelling in British English, but that is beginning to change as people get confused. The computer **disk** is the one we are most likely to come across in the course of our daily routine and so we have become used to this spelling. We now tend to use it outside the world of computers. For example, it is becoming quite usual for people to write:

I have a slipped disk.

See **disc/disk** *under* **Perennial posers** in Chapter 8.

any more/anymore, etc

Expressions such as **any more**, **any place** and **any time** seem to be in the process of change in British English, and this is obviously as a result of American influence on the language.

In American English they are often spelt as one word, for example **anymore,** but the traditional spelling in British English has always separated them into two words, as **any more**.

Nowadays, however, they frequently appear as one word even in British English, so **anymore**, etc. **Everyday/every day** is beginning to go along the same route.

alternate/alternative

There are several other words which are showing signs of being affected by American English. For example, the Brits are beginning to use **alternate** in its American sense of 'offering a choice or a second possibility', as in:

> *We need to come up with an alternate venue in case the one we really want is not available.*

Traditionally in British English this should be **alternative**. *See* **Perennial posers** in Chapter 8.

STILL TWO SEPARATE LANGUAGES

It is not at all surprising that British English has been influenced by American English. America has a powerful influence on the world generally and many foreign students now learn American English rather than British English. What is surprising is that the two languages have remained quite far apart despite the globalization of communication.

Britain still has **pavements** while America has **sidewalks**. Britain still has **bonnets** and **boots** in cars while America has **hoods** and **trunks**. In Britain a **vest** is something you wear under a shirt or other top (known as an **undershirt** in America) while in America it is worn over a shirt and under a jacket (mostly known as a **waistcoat** in Britain). A **nappy** is still a **nappy**, rarely a **diaper**, a **chemist** might be a **pharmacy** but not a **drugstore**, and a **motorway** has not become an **expressway** – and not just because the term is hardly appropriate given the incidence of traffic hold-ups in Britain. Even relatively new inventions have gone their different linguistic ways, so British English has **mobiles** while American English has **cell phones** (or **cells**).

However, things are beginning to pick up pace and more and more American English words are finding their way to British shores. **French fries** have made it across the Atlantic to Britain, and the British **lift** is sometimes known by its American name, **elevator**. The British **lorry** is now quite often called a **truck**, an **aerial** is frequently called an **antenna** and **films** are becoming **movies**.

Increasingly this trend is fast becoming a two-way process and British words are also crossing the Atlantic with more and more Britishisms being spotted in American English. The writer Ben Yagoda, whose blog can be found at britishisms.wordpress. com, is collecting examples of them. The globalization of our media and social media seems to be having an impact: British words like **ginger, snog, trendy, afters, trainers, fortnight, peckish** are appearing more and more regularly in American texts.

Anything could happen in the future. But the major differences between the two languages have lasted a long time.

CHANGES IN GRAMMAR

In terms of vocabulary, the English language has certainly not stood still. The same is true in other areas of the language, although the changes may not be so numerous. One of these areas is grammar.

In the latter part of the 19th century much emphasis was placed on the importance of the rules of grammar and punctuation. In British schools a lot of time was spent on trying to get these rules into the heads of pupils. It was very easy to get things wrong, especially because some of these rules were difficult to understand. However, around the middle of the 1960s, the educational establishment started to feel that these rules were less important.

Those in charge of the curriculum decided that too much attention was being paid to the rules of grammar and punctuation and that these were being too rigidly applied. This, they claimed, was stifling the creativity of young writers. If the emphasis on grammar and punctuation was greatly reduced, then full rein could then be given to the imagination of budding writers. Who knew what literary gems might emerge when the imagination was unfettered by worrying about grammar or punctuation? We could become a nation of prize-winning writers.

Then it eventually became clear that creativity, unless exceptionally inspired, was not enough. Grammar has been variously described as the building blocks of language and the cement that binds words together. It gives structure to sentences and without it they tend to fall apart. Sometimes it might seem to you that we have too many laws in our society, but try living without them and you might well soon want them back. This is what happened to grammar and in time people did want it back.

This was a good idea in principle but it was not so easy to achieve. Grammar was something that pupils had to work really hard at. To bring it back was going to be difficult.

The trouble was that, by the time it was realized that a knowledge of grammar had played a valuable role in writing, there were a great many people around who knew little about it. Teachers who were faced with teaching it had not themselves been taught it to any great extent.

When eventually the importance of grammar was once again recognized, it returned in a less restrictive form. Some of the old rules and conventions were forgotten or set aside, or became more relaxed. Obviously, this led to changes in perception about what was grammatically acceptable and what was not.

SPLIT INFINITIVE

One of these changes involved the **split infinitive**. Now, depending on your age, you may not have encountered the expression, or you may have encountered it but not known what it was or why it could be a problem. Whole generations have been brought up without having the facts about the split infinitive drummed into them, whereas previous generations had been told that it was one of the most important rules of grammar.

There are still quite a few die-hards of an older school of thought who regard it almost as a grammatical sin to split an infinitive. The battle still rages, although many now have no idea of what it is all about.

A split infinitive occurs when the infinitive or base form of a verb has an adverb or adverbial phrase put between the word to and the relevant verb. A much quoted example is to boldly go, from the introduction to the TV series *Star Trek*. If you are determined to avoid splitting the infinitive you have to say boldly to go or to go boldly.

The problem with avoiding splitting infinitives is that you can end up with a piece of written English that sounds unnatural, stilted or with a meaning that is altered.

For example, the sentence

He went home to quietly think about his options.

means the man is thinking about things in a reflective, contemplative way. If we rewrite the sentence as

He quietly went home to think about his options.

we are talking about the quiet manner in which he travelled home. If we rewrite this sentence as

He went home to think quietly about his options.

it reads better than the last one, but what was so hard to understand about the first usage? It's hard to come up with a sensible reason why any usage should be forbidden if it is clear and understandable.

It takes a long time for grammar changes to work their way through the system, but I think we can safely say that the rule against the split infinitive has had its day.

SENTENCES ENDING IN A PREPOSITION

Another grammatical rule that used to be rigidly adhered to was that **sentences must not end in prepositions**. At one point this was such a rigid rule that it has been said that the only thing some people knew about prepositions was that they should not be put at the end of sentences. The rule harks back to Latin, because a Latin sentence cannot end in a preposition. However, this did not mean that English had to follow suit.

This rule is now regularly broken and in fact nowadays most people do not see much point in it. As is the case with avoiding the splitting of infinitives, avoiding putting a preposition at the end of a sentence or clause can easily lead to written language sounding unnatural and stilted, as in:

> *This is the kind of bullying behaviour up with*
> *which the school should not put.*

As for spoken English, it is difficult to imagine someone trying to get their tongue round such a mouthful.

Admittedly, this is quite an extreme example and it is a paraphrase of Winston Churchill's alleged reaction to people who insisted on going to extraordinary lengths to avoid ending a sentence with a preposition:

> *This is the sort of English up with which I will not put.*

The most acceptable and sensible thing to do with regard to prepositions is to put them where they sound most natural. You might say or write:

> *What on earth are the children up to?*

> *There's nothing you can do to prevent it, so it's just*
> *not worth fretting about.*

Sometimes the best place to place a preposition depends on whether the context is formal or informal. In ordinary informal contexts you would write or say:

> *Which hotel did you stay in?*

In a formal written context you might choose to write:

> *In what hotel did you stay?*

There is a lot more to learn about prepositions than worrying about whether to end a sentence with them. For more information about them *see Chapter 4.*

OTHER USAGE CHANGES

who/whom
Another example of modern usage deviating from a previous strict grammatical ruling concerns **whom** and **who**. According to the rules of grammar, **whom** is used as the *object* of a verb or preposition, and **who** is used as the *subject*.

In modern usage, however, **who** is increasingly being used instead of **whom** except in very formal contexts, as in:

Who did he give his old car to?

See also **Perennial posers** in Chapter 8.

will/shall

Here is another pair of words in which a grammatical change has occurred. They are the verbs **will** and **shall**, which are used to form the future tense. Formerly the verb **shall** was always used with I and we, and **will** was always used with you, he/she/it and they. There was an exception to this. **Will** was used with I and we, and **shall** was used with the other personal pronouns when a firm intention was being expressed, as in:

'You shall go to the ball,' said the fairy godmother to Cinderella.

In modern usage **will** is now commonly used in most relevant contexts. *See under* **Perennial posers** in Chapter 8.

'll

Will and **shall** now often appear in the contracted form **'ll**, as in:

I'll go with you.

They'll get the information tomorrow.

The only thing that is new about this is that this contracted form was formerly found only in spoken English, or in very informal written English. Nowadays, in accordance with the new spirit of informality that has spread through the language, this contracted form is used in some more formal contexts. It should still be avoided in the most formal contexts.

can/may

The use of **can** and **may** has also been part of a major change. Formerly there was a clear distinction between the use of **can** (meaning 'be able to') and **may** (meaning 'be allowed to'). Nowadays **can** has taken over from **may** in this meaning and **may** is only used in formal contexts. Thus, people commonly say

> *Can I have a look at that?*

instead of

> *May I have a look at that?*

This is one of those changes in grammar that occurred because many people simply did not understand the difference. Many people opposed the change but could not, in the end, prevent it. *See under* **Perennial posers** in Chapter 8.

try to/try and

As time has gone on, **try and** is one of those expressions that has gained acceptability and at least a degree of respectability. Formerly language purists looked down their noses at it and regarded it as a mistake for **try to**. Now, for the most part the two expressions are widely considered to be interchangeable, with many people preferring **try and** except, perhaps, in the most formal contexts.

See also **Perennial posers** in Chapter 8.

And and But

It is no longer considered an error to start a sentence with **And** or **But**. This is quite a recent change and one that has probably arisen because people started to ask why not. However, do not overdo it. Starting a sentence with **And** or **But** is best kept for those occasions when you want to draw particular attention to something or to emphasize something. A whole string of sentences starting in this way is going to sound very tedious and suggest a lack of talent or imagination in the writer.

hanged/hung

The distinction between these parts of the verb to **hang** is fading quite fast. Many people would now say

> *He was the last criminal in the country to be hung.*

instead of

> *He was the last criminal in the country to be hanged.*

although it is the latter version that is correct in traditional grammar.

Traditionally **hung** should be used in such contexts as:

They hung their coats on the washing line to dry.

See **hanged/hung** *under* **Variable verbs** in Chapter 8.

DESEXING GRAMMAR

The movement to get rid of **sexism** in vocabulary was far-reaching and it had a very important effect on grammar. *See* **Desexing the language** in Chapter 6.

Rules had to be broken and this aroused a lot of opposition. So what were the problems? Some are discussed in the section below.

GETTING RID OF SEXISM

each and every

One of the problems concerned words such as **each** and **every**. It was one of the established rules of grammar that **each**, used either as an adjective (or as a determiner as it is now known) or a pronoun, should be accompanied by a singular verb, as in:

> *Each student will be given a locker key before the swimming lesson.*

> *It's difficult to make a choice because each seems equally suitable.*

The same was true of the adjective or determiner **every**. It, too, had to be accompanied by a singular verb, as in:

> *Every worker is to be given a share of the company profits.*

So far so good. The trouble was that **each** and **every** were always accompanied by a personal pronoun in the singular, where this was relevant. And this takes us back to sexism again. In the days when people saw nothing wrong in assuming that everyone was male, unless it was made absolutely clear that this was not the case, sentences such as

> *Each student was given his own locker key before the swimming lesson.*

and

> *Every worker was given his share of the company profits.*

were the norm. All that has changed, and you can now write

> *Each student was given their own locker key.*

and

> *Every worker was given their share of the company profits.*

See **his and their** and **him and them** below.

everyone/everybody/no one

The same was true of the pronouns **everyone, everybody** and **no one**. If you were acting in accordance with the correct rules of grammar you had to say or write:

> *Students must make their own way to the station on the morning of the trip and everyone has to bring his own lunch.*

Now you can write, without committing a grammatical sin:

> *everyone has to bring their own lunch.*

See **his and their** and **him and them** below.

his and their

Not so long ago there was a distinct male bias in grammar. It was assumed that everyone was male, unless it was known that this was definitely not the case. Words such as student and worker were, therefore, accompanied by **his**, where relevant. The use of **his** indicated the person involved was male, but why should a student or a worker, or anyone else for that matter, be assumed to be male unless there was clear proof of this?

Various ways round the problem of getting rid of sexism while retaining grammatical accuracy were tried out. People tried dropping **his** in favour of **his or her** or **his/her**, but found this awkward and clumsy, as in:

> *Each student was given his or her locker key before the swimming lesson.*

> *Every worker was given his/her share of the company profits.*

Of course, you can sometimes avoid both sexism and grammatical inaccuracy of this kind by putting such sentences in the plural, as in:

> *All of the students were given their locker key before the swimming lesson.*

> *All the workers were given their share of the company profits.*

However, this is not always possible and eventually what was previously said to be completely unacceptable became accepted. The word **his** in such cases came to be replaced by **their**, although this use was ungrammatical. What was previously a serious grammatical error began to appear in reference books and school textbooks.

Sentences such as the following became acceptable:

> *Every worker was given their share of the company profits.*

Who would have thought it? Grammar had lost out to anti-sexism in language. Of course, this did not happen overnight or without a fight, and there are still many people who would never dream of going against grammar rules in this way.

he and him

There was a similar problem concerning the use of the word **he**. Before people began to protest against sexism in language it was common to use the masculine personal pronoun **he** to refer to a noun where the gender was not known, as in:

> *If a student is accepted for the course he will receive an application form in the post.*

It was also common to use the masculine personal pronoun **him** where appropriate, as in:

> *If we find that an athlete has taken drugs we will
> disqualify him.*

The use of **he** and **him** in such contexts became unacceptable
to those who were intent on stamping out sexism in language.
The use of **he or she** and **him or her** or **he/she** and **him/her**
proved too clumsy for many people's tastes and, once again, an
ungrammatical use won the day.

They is often now used to replace **he** where appropriate, as in:

> *If a passenger misses a connecting flight they will be
> compensated.*

While **them** is often used to replace **him** where appropriate, as in:

> *Should an applicant be unsuccessful we will let
> them know immediately.*

got/gotten

British English is beginning to be influenced by **gotten**, the
American past participle of the verb **got**. **Gotten** is often used in
American English instead of **have got**, which is still standard use
in British English. *See* **got/gotten** in Chapter 8, page 196.

INFORMALITY

A general air of increased informality has come over the English
language. This probably began after the end of the Second
World War and was to gather speed, admittedly gradually, as the
decades rolled by. After the end of the war, society changed and
more attention was paid to the ordinary person, rather than just
to members of the upper classes and upper middle classes. This
change to a greater informality speeded up in the 1960s.

Radio became very popular and soon local radio stations began
to develop. The presenters of the programmes issued by these
often used language in a much less formal way than the average
BBC newsreader who spoke with very upper-class accents.

Programmes such as phone-ins also gave ordinary people the
chance to be heard. Listeners heard people using the language
that they themselves used and in their own familiar accents.

Sometimes what they were saying was ungrammatical and sometimes it was slang, but people were using it when they were speaking in public. The language of the broadcast was no longer the preserve of the educated upper and middle classes. It was for everyone.

This air of informality became even more marked when the computer began to make its mark on our lives, and even more marked again when electronic forms of communication became the norm. The use of emails and, to an even greater extent, the use of texting, brought a greater informality to communication and this included punctuation and grammar as well as vocabulary.

Before all this and relatively recently, ordinary people used to compose their written communications mainly by hand. They would send written letters to family and friends even after telephones became commonly used. This was true even of rather formal letters such as letters of complaint.

Business letters in firms were typed, usually by someone specifically employed to do that. Not many ordinary people typed. However, typing on a computer keyboard with a large screen in front of you is much easier than typing on a traditional typewriter. Soon many people were trying their hand at it and, in time, sending emails as a routine way of communicating with people, whether this communication was formal or informal.

Communication by email has had an important effect on the use of language in various ways. It has made some people more careless about spelling, grammar and punctuation. They rely on spell- and grammar-checkers on their computers to alert them to any errors. But these should come with a warning. For example, spell-checkers will indicate that you have written 'thier' instead of 'their' because 'thier' is a misspelling, however, they will not alert you to the fact that you have written 'their' instead of 'there' because both are actual words, though they mean different things. You still have to know how to spell and use grammar.

Emails have also increased the informality of all aspects of writing. Technological advances seem to have increased the speed at which we live generally. We need to do everything very quickly just to keep up with our schedules.

There seems to be a pressure to get emails written as quickly as possible in the expectation that you will somehow get a rapid reply. The process of instant messaging has only increased this feeling, and this need for speed has resulted in an increase of informality, and sometimes carelessness.

OMITTED PUNCTUATION

Thus writers of emails have a tendency to avoid things that might make their task longer. So they miss out commas when actually they should be there, and omit full stops when they definitely should be there. On the other hand, many senders of emails are particularly fond of the dash, which many of them overuse. For more information on punctuation *see* **Punctuating Properly** in *Chapter 2.*

CONTRACTED FORMS

People tend to use contracted forms even in relatively formal emails. So we find a much higher occurrence of words such as **I'll, he'll, you'll, work'll, John'll** and **Mary'll** than was formerly the case. Likewise, we find the contracted forms **don't, didn't, won't, haven't, hadn't, could've** and **should've** used with increasing frequency. Not only that, but the apostrophe is often omitted. This is partly because people are in too much of a hurry to stop and insert it, and partly because they have no idea where it should be inserted. *See* **could of** and **should of** on page 176.

GREETINGS

When people first began to write emails there was a feeling of unease about how to start an email and how to finish it off. There seemed no point in putting the postal address at the top since this was not really relevant. Anything requiring that kind of information would be sent by what became known as 'snail mail'.

There was not such a problem if you knew the person well and were on first-name terms with them. You would continue to write **Dear John,** etc, at the beginning and would sign off with whatever informal greeting you were in the habit of using if you wrote them a note or letter.

However, this was to change also. Things were to get more informal. People started to write **Hi John** instead of **Dear John**, etc. If this seemed too informal, they took to writing simply **John**. Alternatively, they could omit a greeting altogether and simply begin the email. This practice became particularly popular if a series of communications was exchanged in the same day.

People still write **Dear Mr Smith/Ms Jones**, etc, as the opening greeting of a more formal letter, but it is by no means uncommon for such letters simply to begin with the person's name, as in **Mr Smith/Ms Jones**.

The closing greetings of formal letters have been subject to greater change. Formal letters often used to end with **Yours faithfully**. This was quite a curious thing, as there seems no reason for people to swear fidelity to people they either did not know or did not know well. The alternative to this was **Yours sincerely**, although there seems no need to pledge your sincerity either. Nowadays **Yours faithfully** is fading fast in all but the most formal letters and, to some extent, **Yours sincerely** is taking over, although it is still fairly formal.

If you want to do away with suggestions of fidelity and sincerity and still remain fairly formal, you can opt for a greeting such as **Regards** or **Kind regards**. Some people prefer to opt for **Best wishes** or to reduce this just to **Best** and **All Best**.

If you want to choose something much more informal I am sure that you will have some ideas of your own. If you run out of inspiration there is always **Cheers!**

SLANG AND COLLOQUIALISMS

There are many contexts, apart from emails, relating to the Internet where informality has become common. On social-networking sites and blogs people are very likely to use informal punctuation and grammar and vocabulary. They are also likely to use colloquial or slang vocabulary. Strictly speaking, the distinction between colloquial or informal English and slang is that slang is slightly further along the path of informality than colloquial and informal English. However, this distinction is sometimes difficult to discern and there can be a degree of confusion about the whole thing. At any rate, you will find people writing a great deal of non-formal English in emails and on social-networking sites, etc, whether it is colloquial or slang.

Many people seem to think that slang is a 'here today, gone tomorrow' kind of language. But there are a great many slang words that have had a very long shelf-life indeed. Take **skint** for example. It is still alive and kicking, and still means 'having hardly any money', and it goes back to 1925. Mind you, there are always a great many people who are **skint** – they are always with us. Perhaps that has something to do with the survival of the word!

What is unusual is that such words as **skint** are being used much more freely than they ever were before. The same is true of words such as **pissed-off**, meaning 'irritated' or 'annoyed', which has probably been around since the Second World War. **Pants** is a slang term of disapproval which came into being around 1995, much to the delight of adolescents, young and old.

How slang words arise is interesting. There is often a general assumption that they have all come from America, but this is not always the case. Some of them have quite unusual origins. Take **minging** or **mingin** for example. This word has recently enjoyed a great deal of popularity, much featured on the Internet. However, it is far from new.

Mingin is an old Scots word and is derived from the Scots verb *ming*, meaning 'to give off such a strong and unpleasant smell that it makes you want to hold your nose'. Mingin in Scots means having a very unpleasant smell. Around the mid 1980s it began to be used by some Scottish schoolchildren as a general term of disapproval, nothing to do with bad smells. For example, '*A mingin teacher*' was just a teacher that was considered to be no good.

Much later **mingin** or **minging** became widely used as a slang term throughout the UK, particularly among the young. It has taken on a wide range of meanings such as 'disgusting', 'unpleasant', 'unattractive' or 'of poor quality'. You can use it of anyone or anything that you dislike. If you want to insult a person even further you can call them '*a mingin minger*'.

THE DECLINE OF DICTIONARIES

Slang words which have demonstrated a significant degree of longevity have long been admitted to the pages of dictionaries. Mind you, a lot of people might not have realized that. Fewer people now look up large desk dictionaries or other reference books. If they want to check that they have used the correct word in a piece of writing, they are more likely to Google it or look it up on an electronic dictionary. Often they trust to luck, or possibly their memory, and neither of these may be very reliable. Words that are easily confused are even more likely to be confused and, in this culture of speed and informality, there is a lot of room for ambiguity.

This is sad news for dictionaries. In the early part of the 20th century they were regarded as an undisputed authority on language. Many families would have one, and usually only one, and this would often be referred to as 'the dictionary'. People would only change their dictionary when it lost its cover and fell apart. New editions were produced at a far slower rate than they are today and of course there was no Internet to refer to.

Often several decades elapsed before a new edition of a dictionary was published and, during that time, no new additions and changes were recorded where the average person could access them. There was a general feeling that language was set in stone and had to remain that way.

In the late 1970s publishers began to issue new editions of their dictionaries at much shorter intervals and many more publishers began to get involved in dictionary publishing. There was so much competition in this market that the early 1980s brought a phenomenon called the 'dictionary war'.

This increase in dictionary publishing was partly owing to the fact that computerization made it much easier to produce new dictionaries or new editions of dictionaries. This meant that dictionaries could react quite speedily to the changes that were taking place in the language.

The press got involved and helped to popularize dictionaries and indeed began to have some influence on them. Journalists were really mostly interested in rather quirky words that they thought would appeal to their readership, rather than in the many new technical words that were coming into the language. It has to be admitted that dictionary publishers made the most of this situation and some of them played to the gallery, or rather to the media. They deliberately included frivolous words and expressions which at other times would not have stood a chance of being included in a formal dictionary. So it was that expressions such as *yummy mummy* found their way into dictionaries.

This made the task of the traditional lexicographer (a compiler of dictionaries) more difficult. Finding enough space to include the many words that were crying out to be allowed entry to the dictionary was a long-running problem. Taking a word out was not really an option, because who knew when it might pop up again after a period of disuse?

The online dictionary changed things. Lack of space was no longer the problem that it once was in the printed dictionary, and lexicographers had more leeway in their choice of what to include. They could indulge themselves a bit more and demonstrate the growing informality of the language. More and more buzz words were considered suitable candidates for online dictionaries, when in the old days, when 'the dictionary' was still Bible-like in its authority, they would never even have been considered for entry.

2

PUNCTUATING PROPERLY

PUNCTUATION THEN AND NOW

In the latter part of the 19th century much emphasis was placed on the importance of punctuation. In UK schools a lot of time was spent on trying to educate pupils on the many rules of punctuation. It was very easy to get things wrong. However, around the middle of the 1960s, punctuation fell out of favour with the educational establishment. The same thing happened to grammar. *See* Chapter 1, **The Changing Face of English**.

Those in charge of the school curriculum decided that too much attention was being paid to the rules of punctuation and that these were being too rigidly applied. This, they claimed, was stifling the creativity of young writers. If the emphasis on where and if you put a full stop, comma, etc, was greatly reduced, then full rein could be given to the imagination of budding writers. They could just let their story flow – a bit like a stream of consciousness novel although, hopefully, not so long or so complex.

It was certainly a good idea to reduce the number of rules and get rid of much of the rigidity associated with such rules, but there was a downside. Pupils were left not knowing the basics of punctuation.

Why did this matter, and what use is punctuation? Punctuation helps make sense of language and gives it structure. It breaks up what might be a rambling, fairly meaningless piece of writing and makes it into a meaningful unit.

It eventually became clear that creativity, unless exceptionally inspired, was not enough. It was acknowledged that some structure was necessary and punctuation was brought in from the cold, although the rules were never to be so extensive or so rigidly enforced as before.

The rules became even more relaxed when electronic forms

of communication became the norm. The use of emails and, to an even greater extent, the use of texting brought a greater informality to communication and this included punctuation as well as vocabulary and grammar. This relaxed form of punctuation is much easier to get right but there are still some potential pitfalls. These have to be avoided, at least when you are writing some kind of formal communication such as an essay or a business letter. *See Chapter 1.*

COMMON ERRORS IN PUNCTUATION

APOSTROPHE

THE APOSTROPHE SHOWING POSSESSION

The apostrophe (written as ') has' two main uses: to indicate possession, i.e. that something belongs to someone; and to show that there are missing letters or spaces in a contracted word, as in *can't, haven't* and *isn't.*

When indicating possession, an *s* is added after the apostrophe for singular words and for plurals that don't already end in an –*s*. For example, *a girl's bike, a person's right, John's car, the company's premises, the children's school, women's rights.* If a plural word ends in an –*s*, the apostrophe follows the *s* and no extra *s* is added, as in *students' dictionary, employees' contracts.*

If a person's name ends in an *s, x* or *z* sound or the silent French *s* in words like Descartes, then the accepted modern usage to show possession is, most of the time, to add *'s* as in Descartes's Meditations, *Charles's wife, Camus's novel, Francis's birthday.* It is slightly old fashioned to use the apostrophe alone. However in biblical or classical texts it might seem more appropriate as in *in Jesus' name, Herodotus' works.* Use the sound of the end of the word as a guide too. If adding *'s* makes the pronunciation of longer words harder then it's acceptable to just use an apostrophe as in *Williams' latest singles victory.* Follow a consistent style within the text.

It would be foolish to claim that use of the apostrophe is easy, and it is the cause of a great many punctuation errors. What complicates the issue is that it involves knowing quite a lot about the formation of plurals in English, itself a difficult subject because of the number of plurals that are irregularly formed. *See* Chapter 3 which provides information on irregular plural nouns.

COMMON ERRORS WHEN THE APOSTROPHE INDICATES POSSESSION

- Inserting an apostrophe when there is no suggestion that possession is involved, and no contracted forms are involved. This is a particularly common error and there are examples of it all over the place, particularly in shop windows, informal advertisements and menus. For example, you might see the following on a sign outside a fruit and vegetable sign: *fresh local leek's, new potatoes' for sale* or *try these juicy tomatoes'.*

    The vegetables do not own anything and the apostrophes are completely wrong. They should be omitted.

- Inserting an apostrophe where none should be when this relates to such expressions as *sports coach* and *games teacher.* Again, there is no suggestion of possession being involved and to write *sports' coach* or *sport's coach* and *games' teacher* or *game's teacher* is wrong.

- Putting the apostrophe in the wrong place in plural and singular words. Someone may wrongly write *the boys' favourite hobby* when only one boy is involved (it should be *the boy's favourite hobby*), or *the worker's living quarters* when several workers are involved (so it should be *the workers' living quarters*).

    The above error is all the more common with regard to irregular plural forms that do not end in the letter *s*. Instead of writing correctly *women's athletics* and *children's literature* some people wrongly write *womens' athletics* and *childrens' literature. See* Chapter 4 which provides information on irregular plural nouns.

- Putting an apostrophe on such personal possessive pronouns as *hers*, *its* or *theirs.* They show possession and they may end in **s** but they never contain an apostrophe.

Do not write:

These books are theirs'.

or

These books are their's.

The correct form is:

These books are theirs.

- Using **it's** instead of **its** to indicate possession. This is one of the most common errors involving an apostrophe. **Its** should not contain an apostrophe in such sentences as:

  The dog has lost its (not it's) *ball.*

  The cinema had put its (not it's) *prices up, so they found that they did not have enough money with them for popcorn too.*

The word *it's* is only used as a contracted form of *it is*, as in:

  It's unusual to find a very stylish car that is economical to drive too.

See also **The apostrophe in contracted forms** on the next page.
- Using **you're** instead of **your** to indicate possession. This is a very common error. **You're** should not be used in such sentences as:

  Does that answer your (not you're) *question?*

You're is a contracted form of *you are* and should only be used in such sentences as:

  I'm sure you're (not your) *wrong.*

See also **The apostrophe in contracted forms** below.
- Omitting the apostrophe for the sake of appearance when one should be inserted. It is quite common for people involved in advertising or design to want to omit the apostrophe in a word on a book cover, etc, because they feel that it looks cleaner and less cluttered without it. Do not try doing this in an application for a job!

THE APOSTROPHE IN CONTRACTED FORMS

The apostrophe is also used to show the omission of letters in contracted forms, as in *can't* for *cannot*, *isn't* for *is not*, *haven't* for *have not* and *you'll* for *you will*.

COMMON ERRORS WHEN THE APOSTROPHE IS USED IN CONTRACTED FORMS

- Omitting the apostrophe where there should be one. Punctuation may be becoming more informal and relaxed and you may not bother with apostrophes if you are dashing off a text to a friend, but you must put them in if you are writing a formal letter. The use of the apostrophe in this context is one that may well fade over the years, but, for the moment, it is still very much alive.
- Omitting the apostrophe in **it's**, the contracted form of **it is**, as in:

  It's (not its) *not my fault that Dad's car got damaged.*

  This use should not be confused with the use of *its* to show possession when there should be no apostrophe, as in:

  The hamster is sleeping in its cage.

  See pages 41 and 229.
- Omitting the apostrophe in **you're**, the contracted form of **you are**, as in:

  You're (not your) *going to get into trouble if you're late again.*

  This use should not be confused with the use of *your* to show possession as in:

  It was your fault that we were late.

  See **The apostrophe showing possession** on page 39.
- Using an apostrophe when indicating the end of a decade. Since it's simply a plural, you should write *1990s*, not *1990's*.

BRACKETS

Brackets, especially round brackets, occur in pairs and are used to enclose information that is additional to a main statement. They can often be removed without altering the basic meaning of the statement, as in:

> *The student was very rich (richer than anyone his age had any right to be) and that alone made him very popular with many of his fellow students.*

COMMON ERRORS INVOLVING BRACKETS

- Forgetting to insert the second one of a pair of brackets.
- Overusing brackets. Avoid doing this. Too many of them really interrupt the flow of what you are writing. Take time to reorganize what you want to say rather than relying on a lot of brackets to add extra information as you go along.

CAPITAL LETTER

The capital letter has suffered a decline because of the rise in electronic communication. If you are sending someone an email or using your mobile phone to text them it is much easier and quicker to type lower-case letters than capital letters. So it is that a lot of electronic communications go on their merry way with the first person singular pronoun being spelt *i* rather than *I*. Also you will find people's names spelt with an initial lower-case letter instead of a capital letter, as in *peter* and *mary*, and names of places spelt in a similar fashion, as in *rome* instead of *Rome* and *tower bridge* instead of *Tower Bridge*.

Do not be too cheered up by this news. You are not off the hook. We are not witnessing the general collapse of the capital letter. It is still very much alive in more formal contexts, whether these take the form of electronic communication or snail mail.

TIPS REGARDING CAPITAL LETTERS

- Do not forget to put a capital letter as the initial letter of the first word in a sentence, question or exclamation, as in:

Tourists only go there in the summer.

Did you buy tickets for the concert?

Don't do that!

- Do not forget to put a capital letter as the initial letter of a name or proper noun, as in:

  His younger brother's called Michael.

  Stockholm is the capital of Sweden.

  When did the Ice Age begin?

  His birthday is in October.

  What date is Easter Sunday this year?

  She has converted to Buddhism.

- Although the months of the year and the days of the week are spelt with an initial capital letter, the seasons of the year are usually spelt with an initial lower-case letter, as in:

  It's too hot for us there in the summer.

  His favourite season of the year is spring.

  It was a cold and wet autumn day.

  Some people prefer to use an initial capital letter in this context and it is not actually wrong to do so.

- Nouns and adjectives which refer to nationalities or ethnic groups are spelt with an initial capital letter, as in:

  She speaks Spanish fluently.

  It was a conference of French economists.

  However, there is an exception to this. Where an adjective

referring to a nationality is not used literally, it is usually spelt with a lower-case letter, as in:

The brussels sprouts were overcooked.

She walked through the french windows into the garden.

Dogs breeds such as *alsatian* and *chihuahua* don't have to have initial capitals.

- The names of languages are spelt with an initial capital letter, as in:

  She has gone to London to study English.

  But other academic subjects are spelt with an initial lower-case letter, as in:

  He is studying psychology.

- Although the pronoun I is always spelt with a capital letter, the other pronouns are spelt with a lower-case letter, as in *you*, *he*, *she*, *they*, etc, unless they are the first word in a sentence.

- Do not forget to put a capital letter as the initial letter of a trade name, as in:

  He has just bought a Toyota.

  I need to buy a roll of Sellotape to wrap my Christmas presents.

  We used to play Scrabble in the evenings.

- Do not use capital letters simply to emphasize a word, as in:

  Their new house is HUGE.

COLON

Do not avoid the colon. Stop thinking of the colon as something difficult and academic. Using the colon in formal contexts will save you from using the already overused dash. Use it, for example when you are introducing a list of some kind, as in:

> *You will need the following ingredients: eggs, milk,*
> *flour, sugar, cocoa powder and vanilla essence.*

A COMMON ERROR INVOLVING THE COLON

- Do not confuse the colon with the semi-colon. The colon is used to separate two parts of a sentence when the first part leads on to the second part, as in:

> *This area has been significantly upgraded during*
> *the last few years: property prices have soared.*

SEMI-COLON

Do not avoid the semi-colon. Stop thinking of it as something difficult and academic, although it is rather a formal punctuation mark.

COMMON ERRORS INVOLVING THE SEMI-COLON

- Do not confuse the semi-colon with the colon. The semi-colon is used to join clauses that are not joined by a conjunction. The clauses could each be sentences in their own right. It has the force of a strong comma or a dash. The semi-colon is often a useful substitute for a dash.
- The semi-colon is used to separate the items in a long list or a series of things. Do not confuse it with the colon.

    Functioning like a particularly strong comma, the semi-colon is often used in more complicated lists to make them easier to understand, as in:

> *While we are in Edinburgh we plan to visit*
> *Edinburgh Castle; the Canongate area, including*
> *the Palace of Holyroodhouse, Holyrood Park and*
> *the Scottish Parliament; the shops, of course, if we*
> *have any money left from all the sightseeing; the*
> *National Gallery of Scotland and the National*
> *Portrait Gallery.*

COMMA

Punctuation is generally much more informal than it once was and the rules relating to the use of commas are not as rigid as they once were. This is a good thing as the comma has long been a source of confusion to many users of English.

COMMON ERRORS INVOLVING THE COMMA IN LISTS

* Be aware of the following. Commas are often used to separate the various items in lists. Formerly it was considered wrong to put a comma before the *and* which follows the second-last item in a list, as in:

  I bought bread, butter, cheese, grapes and wine.

  Nowadays it is becoming increasingly common in British English, and even more common in American English, to insert a comma in that position, as in:

  I bought bread, butter, cheese, grapes, and wine.

  This comma is known as 'the Oxford comma' or 'the serial comma'. At this stage, whether you use it or not is entirely up to you. However, there are occasions when you should use it to avoid ambiguity. Confusion may arise if the last item in a list of items itself contains the word *and* used in its own right as part of the sentence, as in:

  For the children there was a choice of pizza, chicken nuggets, macaroni cheese and fish and chips.

  For the sake of clarity it is as well to put a comma after the word *cheese*, as in:

  For the children there was a choice of pizza, chicken nuggets, macaroni cheese, and fish and chips.

  Some examples are likely to be found even more ambiguous, as in:

  We had a film marathon and watched The Hobbit, Spider-Man, Avatar and Harry Potter and the Deathly Hallows.

To avoid ambiguity put a comma after *Boys*, as in *Avatar,* and *Harry Potter and the Deathly Hallows*.

If you are dealing with an exceptionally long list of items or with a list in which the items each consist of several words, you should consider using a semi-colon instead of a comma.

• It was formerly absolutely standard practice to separate with a comma the individual adjectives in a list of adjectives placed before a noun, as in:

> *She wore a long, black, low-necked, evening dress.*

It was considered wrong not to do so. That is no longer the case and although it is a relatively new broken rule it is one that is spreading fast. Whether you choose to insert a comma between each of the adjectives in a list is your decision. Be aware, however, that the practice of not inserting commas may become standard practice before too long.

A word of warning if you decide to go on separating adjectives with commas: do not insert a comma before the adjective which comes immediately before the relevant noun when this adjective has an exceptionally close relationship with the noun and, indeed, may help to define it, as shown in the following example:

> *We bought some large, glossy, red peppers to stuff for dinner.*

Do not write:

> *We bought some large, glossy, red, peppers to stuff for dinner.*

Even if you decide to insert commas between the other adjectives, as above, do not separate *peppers* from *red*. The words belong together.

COMMON ERRORS INVOLVING THE COMMA AND CLAUSES

• Where what is known as 'a non-defining relative clause' divides the parts a main clause, this clause is placed within commas. For example, in the sentence

> *Buenos Aires, whose name means 'fair winds', is*
> *the capital of Argentina.*

the clause *whose name means 'fair winds'* is a non-defining relative clause; it doesn't identify the city, it just gives a bit more information, so it could be taken out without altering the essential meaning of the sentence. It is a common error not to insert these commas, as in:

> *Buenos Aires whose name means 'fair winds' is the*
> *capital of Argentina.*

When the relative clause is an integral part of the sentence and not just an extra piece of information, it is called 'a defining relative clause' and there is no need for commas, as in:

> *The restaurant that you mentioned has closed now.*

The clause *that you mentioned* identifies the restaurant, so is essential to understanding the sentence.

- Always remember to include both commas of a pair of commas. This error which relates to commas and non-defining relative clauses involves using only the initial comma to separate off the clause and forgetting to insert the closing one. It is wrong to insert only one comma, as in:

> *Buenos Aires, whose name means 'fair winds' is the*
> *capital of Argentina.*

- Do not use a comma to separate a main clause from a subordinate clause, as in:

> *She was leaving, as he arrived.*

This is wrong. Even when the subordinate clause is placed before the main clause you do not usually need a comma to separate them (although it is not wrong to use one), as in:

> *If it rains we'll have the party indoors.*

However, if the subordinate clause is quite long you should use a comma to separate the different actions for the sake of clarity, as in:

When we had cleaned the windows, hoovered the carpets, polished the furniture and filled some vases with flowers, the room was ready for the party.

- Where there is any risk of confusion you should insert a comma between the subordinate clause and the main clause, especially when the subordinate clause ends with a verb and the following main clause begins with a noun, as in:

If you do not return, the books will be put back on the shelves.

When the students finished painting, their pictures were displayed on the walls.

- It is wrong to insert a comma between a main clause and a subordinate clause beginning with *that*, as in:

I suspected, that she was dishonest.

- Where main clauses are joined by **and,** are quite long and have different subjects, it is a good idea to insert a comma before the **and** for the sake of clarity, as in:

The Olympic stadium has a capacity of 80,000 and houses a nine-lane athletic track, and it will continue to be used as a sports venue for years to come.

When main clauses are joined by *but* users may choose either to use a comma or not to mark off the main clause, but a comma is helpful when both clauses are quite long.

COMMON ERRORS INVOLVING COMMAS WITH ADVERBS OR ADVERBIAL PHRASES

- It was formerly standard practice to use a comma to separate adverbs or adverbial phrases at the beginning of a sentence, such as *however, of course, in the meantime, for example,* from the rest of the sentence, as in:

It's been a pleasant evening. However, it's late and I must go home now.

Nowadays, the comma in this situation is considered optional, but you should insert a comma after the adverb or adverbial phrase if there is any possibility of confusion, as in:

Normally, intelligent adults will appreciate the advantages of the savings scheme.

• It is also a good idea to insert a comma if the adverbial phrase is very long, as in:

After a great deal of careful consideration, I agreed.

COMMON ERRORS INVOLVING COMMAS IN THE ROLE OF BRACKETS

• A pair of commas is often used to separate off a piece of information that is not central to the meaning of a sentence, but is additional to it in the way that bracketed information is. The length of such pieces of additional information can vary from very short to quite long. Do not forget to enclose such information in commas in such situations, as in:

Mark Taylor, the club treasurer, has asked me to address the meeting in his place as he has been unexpectedly called away.

It is quite clear, as you have probably all realized, that the market is not likely to improve in the near future.

Do not forget to include a pair of commas in such situations. One will not be enough.

COMMON ERRORS INVOLVING COMMAS IN VARIOUS OTHER SITUATIONS

• Do not forget to insert a comma between the last word in a piece of direct speech and the closing quotation mark and before the word *say* etc, as in:

'You're late,' she said accusingly.

'The bus is coming,' he called out.

- Do not forget to use a comma to separate a person's name, or the name of a group, from the rest of the sentence when you are addressing them, as in:

  Jim, welcome home!

  I'm over here, Peter.

  I'm sorry, Ms Park, but you have not got the job.

  Gentlemen, let me show you the way.

- Do not forget to insert a comma after an interjection at the start of a sentence, as in:

  Heavens, it's hot!

  See, the display has started.

- Do not forget to use a comma to separate a question tag from the rest of the sentence, as in:

  It was a lovely evening, wasn't it?

  You do still want to go, don't you?

- Remember to insert a comma in numbers that are made up of more than four figures, as in *86,350* and *150,600*. A comma is also often used in numbers consisting of four digits, as in *3,000*, but there is a growing tendency to omit this comma.
- Do not use commas to separate the numbers in dates, as in *1941* and *2013* (not *1,941* and *2,013*).

DASH

- The dash can be used as part of a pair in much the same way as brackets, although dashes are generally much more popular than brackets and used in less formal contexts as in:

  My parents' next-door neighbour – I can't remember his name – has opened a wine bar on the high street.

- The single dash used on its own has several uses, often at the end of sentences, as in:

  I never saw him again – and I wasn't sorry.

  You can keep the book – I've finished with it.

COMMON ERRORS INVOLVING DASHES

- Do not forget to insert the second one of a pair of dashes.
- Do not overuse pairs of dashes. This is a common thing to do as dashes are very popular with a great many writers. Using a lot of dashes is fine if you're just writing a chatty email to a friend, but use them very sparingly in any kind of formal communication. Too many of them really interrupt the flow of what you are writing and can look messy.
- Do not overuse the single dash. As is the case with pairs of dashes, this is a very common thing to do and should be avoided when you are writing any kind of formal communication. To pepper your piece of writing with a lot of dashes looks rather messy.

EXCLAMATION MARK

The exclamation mark is used at the end of a sentence instead of a full stop when the sentence is expressing someone's strong reaction to something, e.g. anger, shock, surprise, as in:

  I absolutely hate him!

The exclamation mark often follows a single word or a group of words without a verb that also express a strong reaction, as in:

  How amazing! Wow!

Exclamation marks may also function as markers of friendly interaction, for example, by making 'Good luck!' seem friendlier than simply 'Good luck'.

A COMMON ERROR INVOLVING EXCLAMATION REMARKS

- Do not overuse exclamation marks. If you do they become ineffective. Restrict their use to situations where very strong reactions are appropriate. Use them very, very sparingly in formal contexts.

FULL STOP

It is a basic requirement of writing to be able to write in sentences. The main function of the full stop is to mark the end of sentence where this does not end in a question mark or exclamation mark.

The full stop is also sometimes used in connection with abbreviations. The modern tendency is to use full stops far less frequently in abbreviations than was formerly the case. Often whether you use them or not is a matter of taste as long as you are consistent within any one piece of writing.

The full stop also plays an important role in email addresses and website addresses.

COMMON ERRORS INVOLVING FULL STOPS

- Full stops are often omitted in error. It is a common error just to leave the end of a sentence without any punctuation at all even though the next sentence may begin with a capital letter, as in:

  I don't know why he left He went away very suddenly without saying anything

  These examples are wrongly punctuated. They should both end with a full stop.

- Failure to recognize the end of a sentence resulting in failure to use the appropriate punctuation, as in:

  He knew he wasn't likely to win the match he hadn't been training as much as usual.

  This is wrong. There should be a full stop after the word match and the he that follows should have a capital letter. Alternatively, there should be a conjunction after match, as in:

> *He knew he wasn't likely to win the match because*
> *he hadn't been training as much as usual.*

- If you find that you have just written a very long sentence, have a careful look at it. Is it correctly punctuated? Should you have broken your piece of writing into more than one sentence and inserted full stops and capital letters where appropriate?
- Omitting the full stop at the end of a group of words complete in itself although it is not actually a sentence, as in:

> *'When did you last see him?'*

> *'Yesterday evening'*

There should be a full stop after the word evening and before the closing quotation mark, as in:

> *'When did you last see him?'*

> *'Yesterday evening.'*

- In dialogue, putting the full stop in the wrong place when it is used with quotation marks. It should go before the closing quotation mark not after, as in:

> *'I'm afraid I can't come with you.'*

- Putting a full stop in abbreviations which involve initial capital letters, such as *BBC*, *TUC*, *USA*, is best avoided. This is not in keeping with modern usage.
- Putting a full stop in abbreviations if one or some of the initial letters do not relate to a full word, such as *TV*.
- Forgetting to insert a full stop where it is needed can prevent an email from reaching its destination or prevent you from accessing a website.

HYPHEN

The hyphen is used in various situations but it has fallen out of favour and is now used much less frequently than formerly. It was once common practice to join two words together as a compound using a hyphen, as in *boat-hook*, *boat-house*, *bake-house*, *boot-guard*, *boot-brush*, *dog-house*, *dog-walker*, *door-handle*, *gun-rack*, *tree-house*.

Now the tendency is to remove the hyphen, making the compound either one word or two. Often this is a matter of taste, although longer words are more likely to become two words than one word.

COMMON ERRORS INVOLVING HYPHENS

* Having made your choice about whether to make a compound noun one word or two, remember to stick with this system throughout any one piece of writing. It is easy to be inconsistent, particularly if you have been undecided about which style to choose.
* Remember that there are some fixed compounds of two or three or more words which still usually retain the hyphen, as in *brother-in-law* and *good-for-nothing*.
* Remember that the hyphen is normally used in compound adjectives before nouns, as in *the wine-producing areas of France*, *a ten-year lease* and *a three-bedroom house*.
* Remember that the hyphen is normally used in compound adjectives where the second element of the compound ends in –ed, as in *fair-minded judges*.
* Remember that the hyphen is normally used in certain adverbs, sometimes to avoid ambiguity, as in *a well-established method*, *a half-organized scheme* and *the best-known writer of travel books about that area*.
* Do not use a hyphen to separate an adverb from an adjective or participle if the adverb ends in –*ly*, as in *a highly successful fashion designer* and *an immaculately dressed young man*.
* Remember that compound numbers such as *two hundred* and *seven thousand* are not hyphenated, although compound numbers from 21 to 99 when written in full are often hyphenated, as in *seventy-five years ago* and *forty-five miles*.
* Be careful when you are using two or more hyphenated compound adjectives which have the same second element and which qualify the same noun. You do not need to repeat

the second element, but you do need to repeat the hyphen, as in *four- and five-storey buildings*.

PARAGRAPH

There is no doubt about it. Paragraphs can be difficult to get to grips with, particularly since they are not governed by any rules which tell us how to deal with them. The good news is that deciding when to start a new paragraph soon becomes a matter of instinct and you do it automatically. Paragraph writing is one of those cases where practice makes perfect – or at least competent. Also, it helps if you read a lot. Seeing how other people do it can be very useful.

COMMON ERRORS INVOLVING PARAGRAPHS

- First of all do remember to arrange your writing in paragraphs if you are writing something that is at all formal. It is all very well to type a rambling email to a friend without worrying about paragraphs, but this approach will not do for college essays, applications for jobs, letters of complaint, etc.
- Do not make your paragraphs too long. The idea behind paragraphs is to make a piece of writing more accessible. If you write very long paragraphs you are going to create the impression of inaccessibility, however good your intentions are.
- It is no longer considered a grammatical sin to have only one sentence in a paragraph, but do not overdo it. Use it occasionally for stylistic effect if you like, but do not end up with a piece of writing consisting of one-sentence paragraphs unless you are a tabloid journalist.

QUESTION MARK

The question mark is used, as you might expect, at the end of a sentence that asks a direct question, as in:

Why did you do that?

Have you seen him lately?

COMMON ERRORS INVOLVING QUESTION MARKS

*   Do not forget to insert a question mark at the end of a question, as in:

    Why are you here.

    There should be a question mark instead of a full stop after *here.*

*   Do not use a question mark when the question is part of reported or indirect speech instead of a question in direct speech, as in:

    She asked me where he was?

    I wondered who told him that?

    Both of these are wrong, because they are examples of reported or indirect speech.

QUOTATION MARKS

Quotation marks are used in pairs and have several uses. They are used to enclose direct speech, i.e. the actual words that someone has spoken, as in:

   'Why on earth did she marry him?' I asked.

They are also used in a piece of writing to enclose a direct quotation from another piece of writing or speech, as in:

   It was a bit of an exaggeration when she referred in her report to 'record-breaking sales'.

They are also sometimes used to indicate titles of books, plays, etc, as in ' *Jane Eyre'*.

Quotation marks in all cases can either be double or single according to taste, as long as this is consistent in any one piece of writing. It is clearer for readers if a different style is used for anything quoted within a quote, so either single quotation marks within double quotation marks or double quotation marks within single quotation marks, as in:

   'It's "business as usual" even though we've got scaffolding up,' the shop manager told us.

COMMON ERRORS INVOLVING QUOTATION MARKS

- Do not omit the second set of quotation marks, as in:

    'We are leaving tomorrow, she said.

- Do not use a single quotation mark followed by a closing double one, as in:

    'Let's meet for lunch next week," he suggested.

3

IRREGULAR PLURAL NOUNS

Irregular plurals refer to the plural form of nouns that do not make their plural in the regular way.

Most nouns in English add –*s* to the singular form to make the plural form, as in *boy* to *boys*. Some add –e*s* to the singular form to form the plural, as in *church* to *churches*. Nouns ending in a consonant followed by –*y* have –*ies* as a regular plural ending. Thus *fairy* becomes *fairies* and *berry* becomes *berries*. The foregoing are all examples of regular plurals.

Irregular plural nouns include nouns that are different in form from their singular forms and do not simply add an ending, such as *men* from *man*, *women* from *woman* and *mice* from *mouse*. Irregular plurals are formed in a number of different ways.

- Some irregular plurals are formed by changing the vowel of the singular forms, as in *feet* from *foot*, *geese* from *goose* and *teeth* from *tooth*.
- Some irregular plural forms are formed by adding **–en**, as *oxen* from *ox* and *children* from *child*.
- Some nouns ending in **–f** form irregular plurals in **–ves**, as in *loaf* to *loaves*, *half* to *halves*, *wife* to *wives* and *wolf* to *wolves*, but some have alternative endings, as in *hoof* to either *hoofs* or *hooves*, and some form regular plurals by simply adding **–s** to the singular form, as in *roof* to *roofs*.
- Some irregular plural forms are the original foreign plural forms of words adopted into English, for example *stimuli* from *stimulus*, *phenomena* from *phenomenon* and *criteria* from *criterion*. In modern usage there is a growing tendency to anglicize the plural forms of foreign words. Many of these coexist with the original plural form, as in *thesauruses* and *thesauri*, *formulas* and *formulae,* and *gateaus* and *gateaux*. Sometimes the anglicized plural formed according to the regular English rules differs slightly in meaning from the

irregular foreign plural. Thus, *indexes* usually applies to the guides to the content at the end of books, and *indices* is normally used in the field of mathematics.

- Some nouns have irregular plurals in that the plural form and the singular form are the same. These include *sheep*, *grouse* (the game-bird) and *salmon*. Also, some nouns have a regular plural and an irregular plural form. Thus, *brother* has the plural forms *brothers* and *brethren*, although *brethren* is now mainly used in a religious context and is archaic in general English.

4

PROBLEMATIC PREPOSITIONS

PREPOSITIONS

You may think that, as parts of speech go, prepositions look fairly harmless. This is probably because many of them are so short (e.g. *in*, *on*, *from*, *off*, *with*, *to*) that you would not think that they could cause much in the way of trouble. However, small is not always innocent. Just think of the discomfort that midges can cause! Prepositions may be short but they are certainly not problem-free.

WHAT FOLLOWS WHAT?

But let's be fair to prepositions. The problems associated with them tend to centre not on the prepositions themselves, but on their relationships. It is the function of prepositions to show how some elements in sentences relate to other elements, and it is not always easy to decide which preposition connects what to what. This is a particular problem for learners of English as a foreign language or as a second language. However, it can also puzzle native speakers.

Some words cause particular problems because they can hook up with more than one preposition. For example, the verb *agree* can be accompanied by *to*, *with* or *on*, while the adjective *responsible* can team up with *to* or *for*. The A–Z list below, although it is by no means comprehensive, will give you guidance on some of these.

absent from/present at

You are said to be **absent from** a meeting or place when you are not there, as in:

> *That is the third day the pupil has been absent from school.*

> *The lead actor was absent from last night's performance because he was ill.*

The opposite of **absent from** is **present at**, as in:

> *There were 300 people present at the protest meeting.*

absolve from

If you **absolve** someone **from** blame you say publicly or officially that they are not guilty of a crime or act of wrongdoing, often one that they have been accused of, as in:

> *He has been absolved from all blame in connection with the accident.*

Absolve from is mostly used in formal contexts.

accustomed to/in the habit of

If you are **accustomed to** something it is something that you do regularly or are very familiar with, as in:

> *Their teenage children were accustomed to the amenities of city life and found life in a country village very boring.*

It is a more formal way of saying 'used to', as in:

> *They were accustomed to sitting about doing nothing and certainly didn't want to start working.*

Another way of saying this is **in the habit of**, as in:

> *She's in the habit of going for a run after work every evening.*

accuse of/charge with

Both of these verbs involve saying that someone is guilty of something, but they are followed by different prepositions.
accuse of
If you believe that someone has done something wrong you can **accuse** them **of** wrongdoing, as in:

> *Money had gone missing from the till and he accused one of his employees of taking it.*

If you use the noun **accusation** this is often followed by the preposition **against,** as in:

> *He appears to have made false accusations against his former business partner.*

charge with

If the police go one step further and formally accuse someone of a crime they **charge** them **with** it, as in:

> *The police charged him with manslaughter.*

If you use the noun **charge** this is often followed by the preposition **against**:

> *The police called the suspected criminal in for questioning then decided to press charges against him.*

adhere to

If you **adhere to** a rule or an agreement you do what it says you should do or in other words you obey it, as in:

> *We expect all pupils to adhere to the school's rules during the school day, with no exceptions.*

Adhere to is mostly used in formal contexts.

afraid of/frightened of

If you are **afraid of** something you feel fear because you think you might be hurt or harmed, as in:

> *The children are afraid of the dark.*

> *She's afraid of dogs because she was bitten by one when she was a child.*

You can also say that you are **frightened of** something, which has the same meaning as **afraid of**, as in:

> *The boy's frightened of ghosts although he's been told that there's no such thing.*

agree

The verb **agree** can be followed by various prepositions according to its meaning.

agree to

If you **agree to** something you say that you will allow it to happen, as in:

> *They agreed to our plan right away.*

If you **agree to** do something you say that you will do it, as in:

> *He agreed to clean the car at the weekend after complaining it wasn't his turn.*

agree with

You are said to **agree with** someone about something if you both have the same opinion or feeling about it, as in:

> *I hardly ever agree with my brother but I think he's right about this.*

If you approve of something, such as a suggestion or a plan, you can be said to **agree with** it, as in:

> *I agree with his proposals for a wind farm but there will be a lot of opposition from the people who live in the area.*

Less commonly **agree with** can be used to indicate that something is good for you, as in:

> *The warmer climate certainly agrees with him and his health has improved dramatically.*

The opposite of this is to **disagree with**, as in:

> *The politicians disagreed with each other about the way forward.*

If you want to use the noun **agreement** in this context this is also followed by the preposition **with**, as in:

> *If we're all in agreement with each other, we can move on to the next issue up for discussion.*

agree on

If people discuss and reach a decision about something you can say that they **agree on** it, as in:

The young couple have finally got their families to agree on a date for the wedding.

alternative/ alternative to

When used to describe a course of action the adjective **alternative** refers to something that can be done or used instead of something else, as in:

The police are recommending an alternative route to the city centre.

Alternative can also be used as a noun taking the preposition **to**, as in:

My mother's always saying that there's no alternative to hard work when it comes to passing exams.

He had no alternative but to cancel his plans after he was called in to work.

analogous to

Something is **analogous to** something else if it is similar in some ways to something else and so able to be compared with it, as in:

These cases of flu are certainly analogous to those that have been described in parts of Europe.

Analogous to is used in formal contexts.

answer

answer for/vouch for

1   If you have to **answer for** something you are responsible for it and have to explain how it came to happen, as in:

The team lost by a huge margin and their manager will have to answer for their appalling performance.

Your brother will have to answer for his bad
behaviour and remain after school hours to see the
headmaster.

2   If you say that you can **answer for** someone's good qualities
or characteristics you mean that you can say with certainty
that they have these, as in:

I have known the young woman for many years
and can answer for her honesty.

Answer for is similar to **vouch for**, as in:

Several people are willing to vouch for the integrity
of the accused.

3   If you say that you **can't answer for** someone else who is not
present it means that you cannot say what they are likely to
think or do, as in:

I'm definitely in favour of the scheme but I can't
answer for any of my colleagues.

answer to
If you **answer to** someone in authority it means that you have to
explain to them why you have acted in the way you did, as in:

I'm not going to tell you why I'm late. I only answer
to the head of the department.

anxious
anxious about
If you are **anxious about** something you are worried about it for
some reason and think about it all the time, as in:

The students are anxious about their exam results.

The child is anxious about travelling on the train
by herself.

anxious to
If you are **anxious to** do something you want very much to do it,
as in:

She is anxious to get a job so she can start saving some money.

They are anxious to help.

anxious for

Anxious for can sometimes be used to mean 'worried about', as in:

Their son is doing a dangerous job and they're anxious for his safety.

However, **anxious for** can also indicate that you want very much to have something or that you want it to happen, as in:

The workers are anxious for an immediate increase in salary.

They are anxious for their house alterations to get finished but the builders are very slow.

apart from

You use **apart** immediately followed by **from** when you are referring to an exception of some kind, as in:

I like all kinds of films apart from horror.

Apart from my sister everyone in our family has summer birthdays.

Apart from can also be used to mean 'as well as', as in:

Apart from their large town house in London they have a flat in Paris and a villa in Spain.

appeal

appeal against

If you **appeal against** a decision or a judgement you ask for it to be reconsidered and changed, as in:

He was found guilty of fraud but his defence team have appealed against the verdict.

Note that in American English **appeal** is used without a preposition following it, as in:

> *They have appealed the verdict.*

appeal to

If you **appeal to** someone for something you make a request for some kind of help, as in:

> *Police have appealed to the public for information regarding the recent break-ins in the area.*

> *Charities for homeless people have appealed to people to give generous donations this winter.*

If something **appeals to** you, you like it and find it attractive or interesting, as in:

> *The idea of getting married at a beach resort really appeals to me.*

> *Living in the city centre just doesn't appeal to me.*

apply

apply for

If you **apply for** something you make a formal request to be considered for something such as a job, a place at college, etc, as in:

> *There's a job vacancy in our department but you have to apply for it in writing by Tuesday of next week.*

apply to

Apply to means 'to concern or affect someone or something', as in:

> *This warning doesn't apply to people who are already respecting the school's rules.*

approve of/disapprove of

If you **approve of** an action, suggestion, etc, you think it is a good thing and are pleased with it, as in:

> *His parents approved of his decision to go to university.*

> *Not all the staff approved of the board's decision to expand the company.*

The opposite of **approve of** is **disapprove of**, as in:

> *Many parents disapprove of the changes in the school curriculum.*

arrive

arrive at/reach

If you **arrive at** a place you come to it after a journey, as in:

> *We arrived at the party just as everyone else was going home.*

Note that the verb **reach** without a following preposition can often be used instead of **arrive at**, as in:

> *We hope to reach the hotel before nightfall.*

arrive in

If the place at the end of your journey is a country or a town you use **in** instead of **at** with **arrive**, as in:

> *The ferry was delayed and we did not arrive in France until after dark.*

> *We will phone you when we arrive in Rome.*

ashamed of

If you are **ashamed of** something you have done you feel guilty or embarrassed because you think it was wrong or unacceptable in some way, as in:

> *He was really ashamed of shouting at his mother last night.*

You can also be **ashamed of** yourself when you feel this kind of guilt, as in:

*He felt ashamed of himself for shouting at his
mother last night.*

ask after

If you **ask after** someone you ask how they are, if they are well,
etc, as in:

*My doctor was at school with my mother and
he always asks after her whenever I have an
appointment to see him.*

attached to

If you are **attached to** someone or something you like them very
much and have often known or owned them for a long time, as in:

The children are very attached to their grandfather.

*She's now a teenager but she's still very attached to
her teddy bear.*

aware of/conscious of/unaware of/unconscious of

If you are **aware of** someone or something you know that they
exist or are present, as in:

She was suddenly aware of footsteps behind her.

*I was aware of an atmosphere of hostility between
them.*

*She was all too aware of the noises in the house
at night because she wasn't used to staying there
alone.*

The opposite of **aware of** is **unaware of**, as in:

*He was quite unaware of the time until he heard
the clock strike midnight.*

The expression **conscious of** means much the same as **aware of**,
as in:

He was conscious of someone staring at him.

> *She was conscious of a change in their attitude*
> *towards her.*

The opposite of **conscious of** is **unconscious of**, as in:

> *He seemed totally unconscious of the fact that*
> *people were laughing at him.*

bank on/rely on/depend on

If you **bank on** something happening you rely on it happening and hope that you will get some advantage from it happening, as in:

> *I'm running late and I'm banking on the train being*
> *late. It usually is.*

> *He's only had time to revise three or four topics for*
> *the history exam and he's banking on there being*
> *questions on at least two of these.*

Bank on is slightly more informal than **rely on**. You can also use **depend on** in this way.

because of/owing to/due to

If something happens **because of** something it happens as a result of it, as in:

> *The football match had to be cancelled because of a*
> *flooded pitch.*

> *Our plane was delayed because of a strike by*
> *baggage handlers.*

The phrase **owing to** is a slightly more formal than **because of**, as in:

> *We had to postpone our holiday owing to my*
> *mother's illness.*

> *Work in the whole factory was brought to a*
> *standstill owing to a serious electrical fault.*

Due to is sometimes used as an alternative to **because of** and **owing to**. Although it is grammatically wrong to do so, this usage is becoming widespread because the difference between **due to** and **owing to** and **because of** is quite difficult to understand. **Due to** is adjectival and means 'caused by', while **because of** and **owing to** are prepositional, as in:

> *Everyone agreed that it was an error due to lack of experience.*

> *Cancellations due to bad weather are expected.*

become of
You use the phrase **become of** to refer to what has happened to someone or what they are doing now, as in:

> *He was at primary school with me and I often wonder what became of him.*

> *We don't know what became of him after he left college.*

begin
begin by
If you **begin by** doing something you do it first before doing anything else, as in:

> *I think we'll begin by putting the kettle on for a cup of tea.*

begin with
If you **begin with** something you deal with it first before carrying out other tasks, as in:

> *Assembly in that school always begins with a prayer.*

believe in
If you **believe in** something such as magic, fairies or ghosts, you feel sure that these exist.

> *The children still believe in Father Christmas.*

The same is true if you **believe in** God, as in:

*She had been raised in a religious household but no
longer believed in God.*

The phrase **believe in** can also be used to mean that you have
confidence and trust in someone and are sure that they will be
successful, as in:

*In her early career she received many rejections
but she continued to believe in herself and went on
to become a famous actress.*

If you **believe in** something can also mean you are in favour of it
or support it because you think that it is right, as in:

*He believed in equality for women long before it
became a popular issue.*

belong to
If something **belongs to** someone, they own it, as in:

That car over there belongs to my neighbour.

If you **belong to** something, such as a club, organization, group or
category, you are a member of it, as in:

They all belong to the local tennis club.

They belonged to the English aristocracy.

benefit from
If you **benefit from** something you get some form of advantage
from it, as in:

*Lower paid workers should benefit from the new
tax rules.*

blame
blame for
If you **blame** someone **for** something you say that they are
responsible for something bad, as in:

*The driver of the other car blamed him for the
accident.*

> *Her boss blamed her for the error in the accounts*
> *although it was really his mistake.*

blame on

The expression **blame** something **on** someone used to be considered unacceptable by many users, but now things have changed and this use has become quite widespread, as in:

> *I wasn't even here when the vase broke. Don't*
> *blame it on me!*

If you want to use the noun **blame** to convey this meaning you say or write:

> *They tried to put the blame on me although I was*
> *completely innocent.*

bored

bored with

If you are **bored with** something you no longer find it interesting, as in:

> *He says he's bored with his job and wants to leave.*

bored of

The expression **bored of** is sometimes used in speech or very informal pieces of writing, as in bored of this programme. It should not be used in more formal writing.

capable of/incapable of

If you are **capable of** something or doing something, you are able to do it or are liable to do it:

> *I really didn't think that he was capable of playing*
> *the piano like that.*

> *She thinks that she's quite capable of moving into a*
> *flat on her own.*

The opposite of **capable of** is **incapable of**, as in:

> *She had thought herself incapable of speaking in*
> *public.*

> *That messy boy seems incapable of tidying up after
> himself!*

Incapable of is often used in quite formal contexts.

care
care for

If you **care for** someone who is sick, disabled, old, very young, etc, you look after them and make sure that they have the things they need, as in:

> *She employs someone to care for her elderly mother
> during the day.*

If you say you **don't care for** something, it means you don't like it, as in:

> *I don't care for red wine.*

It can also be a rather old-fashioned (and rather rude!) way of saying '*No, thank you*', as in:

> *Would you like some fruit cake?*
> *No, I don't care for it.*

care about

If you **care about** something you think that it is important and you are concerned about it, as in:

> *If you cared about the environment you would
> recycle more of your household rubbish.*

If you **care about** someone or something you really like them or love them, as in:

> *He asked his mother to come and stay with them
> because he really cared about her.*

This is rather a formal use.

centre
centre on

If something **centres on** something it is the focus or centre of attention or activity, as in:

His political thinking is centred on the redistribution of wealth.

The greater part of the bankers' discussion centred on the downturn in the world economy.

centre around/round

The phrase **centre around** or **centre round** is now frequently used instead of **centre on**. This is disliked by some language commentators on the grounds that the word **centre** is too precise to be used with the imprecise words **round** or **around**. The phrases **centre around** or **centre round** are more likely to be tolerated by precise users if they are used with reference to something generalized rather than something specific, as in:

Most of her hobbies centre around the great outdoors.

charge with *see* **accuse of**

close to *see* **near to**

clothed in *see* **dressed in**

commitment to

If you show **commitment to** someone or something you show loyalty to them, as in:

His commitment to the football team caused him to turn down a lucrative transfer offer.

The expression **be committed to** can have much the same meaning:

She was so committed to her charity work that she spent all her free time volunteering.

communicate

communicate to

If you **communicate** something **to** someone you tell them about it, as in:

> *She had to communicate news of the factory's*
> *closure to the workforce.*

This is used in rather formal contexts.

communicate with

If you **communicate with** someone you exchange information with them, as in:

> *We communicate regularly with each other by email.*

compare

compare to or with

When you compare two things you often do so as a comment on their differences or similarities. In this context you can follow **compare** with either **to** or **with**. Formerly **compare to** was considered incorrect in this context, but the difference between the two phrases was not at all clear to some users. Now things have become simplified and **compare with** and **compare to** are both considered acceptable in this context, as in:

> *It's interesting to compare the school rules with*
> *those of a hundred years ago.*

> *It's a pity for him that he always feels he is being*
> *compared to his older brother.*

compare to

When you are only commenting on the similarity between two things and saying that they are like each other, then **compare to** is the correct phrase, as in:

> *He is a very good actor but you certainly cannot*
> *compare him to Robert de Niro.*

compatible with/incompatible with

If something is **compatible with** something else the two things are able to exist together or can be used together without any problems being caused, as in:

> *Having such a high pressure job isn't compatible*
> *with the demands of family life.*

The opposite of this is **incompatible with**, as in:

> *The new head's approach to education is totally incompatible with the deputy head's approach.*

complain

complain about

If you **complain about** something you think that there is something wrong with it and you say that you are not satisfied with it, as in:

> *The food in the restaurant was so bad that several people complained about it.*

complain of

If you **complain of** something it can mean that you say that you are annoyed or upset about it, as in:

> *The man who was arrested complained of ill-treatment by the police.*

It can also mean that you have a pain in part of your body or that you are feeling ill, as in:

> *The child is complaining of a pain in her stomach.*

complain to

If you **complain to** someone you tell them that you are not satisfied with something or that someone or something has made you annoyed or upset, as in:

> *The radio I bought is faulty and I'm going to complain to the manager of the shop where I bought it.*

> *If the students keep on having noisy parties every weekend we are going to complain to their landlord.*

compliment on

When you **compliment** someone **on** something you say something pleasant in praise of their appearance, ability, etc, to show that you admire them, as in:

> *Several people complimented her on her new hairstyle.*

> *He complimented the young man on his driving skills.*

composed of

If something is **composed of** some parts, substances, people, etc, it is made up of them, as in:

> *The committee is composed of local business people.*

> *The exam is composed of two units: an oral test and a written test.*

The phrase **be composed of** is similar in meaning to that of **consist of**, but it is often used in more formal contexts. *See* **consist of**.

concerned

concerned about or for

If you are **concerned about** something you are worried about it, as in:

> *She is concerned about environmental issues.*

The phrase **concerned for** also means worried about, as in:

> *Many young people are concerned for the future of the planet.*

concerned with

If something is **concerned with** something it deals with it or is about it, as in:

> *The book is concerned with changes in society after the Second World War.*

conditional on

If something is **conditional on** something it means it will only happen or be done if something else happens or is done first, as in:

> *His offer to buy their house is conditional on a substantial reduction in the price.*

> *The price we have quoted is conditional on the order being delivered right on time.*

This phrase in found in fairly formal or commercial contexts.

conducive to

If something is **conducive to** something it makes it possible or more likely to happen, as in:

> *The holiday complex was very noisy and hardly conducive to a relaxing time.*

The phrase **conducive to** is used in fairly formal contexts.

confidence in

If you **have confidence in** someone you feel sure that they are going to do something well or are going to succeed in something that they are trying to do, as in:

> *He has to undergo a long and difficult operation to fix his heart but he has complete confidence in the surgeon.*

confident of

If you are **confident of** something you feel sure that it will happen or that you will achieve it, as in:

> *She says that she is confident of victory because she is by far the better player.*

> *He seems to be confident of getting the job.*

concentrate on

If you **concentrate on** something you give it most of your attention rather than attending to other things, as in:

> *They usually spend a lot of time playing various sports but this term they are having to concentrate on their school work.*

conform to/with

If something **conforms to** something such as a rule or guideline, it obeys or follows it, as in:

> *Planning permission was refused because the plans of the building did not conform to local building regulations.*

You can also use **conform with** in this context, as in:

> *The proposed skateboarding park must conform with safety regulations.*

Conform to can also mean 'to agree with or match', as in:

> *He doesn't conform to my idea of a doctor: he's so young!*

You can also use **conform with** in this context, as in:

> *He certainly did not conform with their idea of the kind of man their daughter should marry.*

connect with/to

When the verb **connect** means 'to join' it can be followed either by **to** or **with**, as in:

> *The proposed road would connect our town with the city.*

> *Our property is connected to theirs by a narrow winding lane.*

If the verb means 'to notice or show a link or relationship between someone or something', **connect** is followed by **with**, as in:

> *Police have failed to connect him with the crime.*

conscious of *see* aware of

consent to

If you **consent to** something, you agree to it or give your permission for it to happen, as in:

> *He was rather surprised when she consented to a trial of his suggested scheme.*

Consent to is more formal than **agree to**.

consist of

If something **consists of** two or more things or people, it is made up of them, as in:

*The football team consists of pupils from two
different schools.*

*The mixture consists of flour, milk, eggs and
flavouring.*

The phrase **consists of** means the same as **be composed of** but it
is not used in the passive.

content
content with
If you are **content with** something you are quite happy or willing
to have it or accept it, as in:

She seems to be content with a very quiet life.

content to
If you are **content to** do something you are happy or willing to do
it, as in:

*He was content to work overtime every week as
long as he got paid for his extra hours.*

contrast with
If two things **contrast with** each other they show a marked
difference when they are compared with each other, as in:

*The children's colourful coats contrasted with the
stark whiteness of the snow.*

convinced of
If you are **convinced of** something you are sure that it's true, as in:

*She was convinced of his honesty despite her
friend's warning.*

cope with
The phrase **cope with** is similar in meaning to **deal with**, but the
situation involved is often more difficult, or more of a problem,
as in:

*She has to cope with a full-time job on top of looking
after her children and elderly parents.*

See **deal with** below.

correspond
correspond to
If something **corresponds to** something it is very similar to or the same as something or it is the equivalent of it, as in:

> *The title of advocate in the Scottish legal system corresponds to the title of barrister in the English one.*

correspond with
If you **correspond with** someone you write letters to them and receive letters from them, as in:

> *They have never met but they have corresponded regularly with each other since they were childhood pen pals.*

critical of
If you are **critical of** someone or something you point out what you regard as their faults or bad points, as in:

> *Several parents were critical of the school's policy towards bullying.*

culminate in
If something **culminates in** something it finishes in that particular way, as in:

> *The evening culminated in an impressive fireworks display, to the delight of the spectators.*

Culminates in is a formal way of saying **ends in**.

deal with
If you **deal with** something or someone you take the necessary action to achieve a result or solve a problem, as in:

> *The manager will deal with the customer's complaint.*

> *Trying to deal with falling sales and increased production costs is extremely difficult.*

If a book, speech, etc, **deals with** a subject it is about that subject, as in:

>   *The article deals with homelessness.*

decide
decide on
To make up your mind about something or to choose someone or something after thinking carefully, as in:

>   *She spent ages worrying about what to wear to the party and finally decided on her little black dress.*

>   *The new graduate had several job offers, but she decided on a career in the family business.*

decide upon
Decide upon has the same meaning as **decide on** but it is often used in more formal contexts.

delight
delight in
If you **delight in** something (often something that upsets someone else) you take pleasure in it or enjoy it, as in:

>   *She delights in watching the sunset from her balcony.*

>   *He delights in teasing his younger brother and making him cry.*

delighted with
If you are **delighted with** something you are very pleased and happy about it, as in:

>   *The girl was delighted with her new dress.*

depend on
If something **depends on** something else it is directly affected by that, as in:

>   *Where we go on holiday this year depends on how much we are prepared to pay.*

If you **depend on** someone or something you need their support in order to survive, as in:

She depends on an allowance from her parents to pay her bills at university.

See **bank on** on page 72.

dependent on
If you are **dependent on** someone you depend on their support for your survival, as in:

He was a student until he was nearly thirty and was dependent on his parents all that time.

The magazine is dependent on local advertising for its survival.

deprive of
If you **deprive** someone **of** something you stop them from having it, especially something that they really ought to have, as in:

The laws are there to stop people being deprived of their rights.

deter from
If something **deters** you **from** doing something it stops you from doing it, as in:

They put a fence round the old tree to deter children from climbing it.

detract from
If something **detracts from** something it makes it seem less good or attractive, as in:

The ruins of the old factory detract from the beauty of the area.

Do not confuse this with **distract from** on page 88.

devoid of

If something is **devoid of** something it is completely lacking in it, as in:

> *The house is comfortable enough but it is completely devoid of style.*

devoted to

If you are **devoted to** someone you love them very much or are very loyal to them, as in:

> *She's devoted to her boss and won't hear a word against him.*

> *She's devoted to her grandchildren and always bakes them special treats.*

different

different from

Different can be followed by the prepositions **from, to** and **than**. In British English **different from** is the most acceptable construction, especially in formal contexts, as in:

> *Her attitude to work was quite different from his.*

different to

Different to is found in informal, especially spoken, contexts, as in:

> *Their lifestyle is completely different to mine.*

This construction should be avoided in formal use.

different than

Different than is frequently used in American English, but this construction is not considered correct in British English, although it is becoming more common. **Different than** is considered more acceptable if it is followed by a clause, as in:

> *It looks no different than it did a decade ago.*

disagree with *see* agree with

disapprove of *see* approve of

disloyal to *see* **loyal to**

dispose of

If you **dispose of** something that you do not want or need any longer you throw it away or give it to someone, as in:

> *You must remember that some things can be recycled when you are disposing of your household waste.*

distract from

If you **distract** someone **from** something you take their attention away from something, sometimes by getting them to pay attention to something else, as in:

> *It's dangerous to talk to the driver because you'll distract him from his driving.*

See also **detract from** on page 86.

dressed in

If you are dressed in something, you are wearing it, as in:

> *The children were all dressed in their school uniform.*

The phrase **clothed in** means the same, but it is usually found in more formal contexts, as in:

> *The king and queen were clothed in scarlet robes trimmed with ermine.*

due to *see* **because of**

end
end in

If something **ends in** something it finishes in that particular way, as in:

> *The night ended in triumph as he took home three awards.*

Culminate in is a more formal way of saying this.
end with

If something **ends with** an event, etc, that event marks the finish of something, often being the last of a series, as in:

> *The choir sang a selection of well-known songs,*
> *ending with the national anthem.*

engaged
engaged in
If you are **engaged in** something you are busy doing something or are very much involved in something, as in:

> *They are engaged in the difficult process of selling*
> *their house.*

Engaged in is usually used in quite formal contexts.
engaged to
If you are **engaged to** someone you have said that you will marry them, as in:

> *Sue has just got engaged to Tom and they are*
> *planning to get married early next year.*

engrossed in
If you are **engrossed in** something you are so interested in it that you concentrate on it and do not notice anything else, as in:

> *She was so engrossed in the film that she did not*
> *hear me when I called to her.*

envious of
If you are **envious of** someone, you wish that you had something that they have or do, as in:

> *She is envious of her brother because he is old*
> *enough to stay out late.*

If you are **envious of** something that someone has, you wish that you had it, as in:

> *They were envious of the luxury house that their*
> *friends lived in.*

escape from

If you **escape from** a dangerous place or situation you succeed in getting away from it, as in:

> *They escaped from poverty by managing to emigrate.*

except

The word **except** introduces the person or thing that a general statement does not apply to, as in:

> *You can borrow any of the books except this one.*

It is sometimes followed by **for**, as in:

> *We will all be there except for Jim.*

with the exception of

When you are mentioning someone or something that is an exception you often use the phrase **with the exception of**, as in:

> *The whole family went with the exception of my aunt, who was feeling ill.*

An **exception** is someone or something that a general statement of some kind does not apply to.

faith in

If you have **faith in** someone, you trust them absolutely or have complete confidence in them, as in:

> *She has great faith in her counsellor.*

If you lose **faith in** someone, you no longer trust them or have confidence in them, as in:

> *The workers are losing faith in their management team and are worried about their jobs.*

faithful to/unfaithful to

If you are **faithful to** someone or something you remain loyal to them and continue to give them your support, as in:

*When the king was defeated in battle most of the
nobles remained faithful to him and helped him to
escape overseas.*

*The politician remained faithful to his principles
and refused to vote with his party on the issue.*

If you are **faithful to** a husband or wife, etc, you are in a
monogamous relationship with them, as in:

*He promised in his wedding vows to be faithful to
his wife.*

The opposite of **faithful to** is **unfaithful to**, as in:

He did not want to be unfaithful to his wife.

familiar
familiar to
If something is **familiar to** you, you know it well, as in:

*Although her face is familiar to me I cannot
remember her name.*

familiar with
If you are **familiar with** something, you know or understand it
well, as in:

*She was brought up in this area so she must be
familiar with it.*

filled with *see* full of

fond of
If you are **fond of** someone you like them very much and may even
love them, but usually not in a romantic way, as in:

They are cousins and are very fond of each other.

*John and the girl next door are very fond of each
other, but there has never been any suggestion of
romance between them.*

free of/ free from

If something or someone is **free of** something they do not have any of it or contain any of it, as in:

> *The room is now free of dust.*

> *The patient is now free of pain.*

The expression **free from** means the same as **free of** and is used in much the same way, as in:

> *Now that the sun has gone down we are free from that terrible oppressive heat.*

> *Yesterday the doctors thought she had measles but today she is free from all the usual symptoms.*

friend

friends with

If you are **friends with** someone that person is your friend, as in:

> *I have been friends with Anne since our schooldays.*

friendly with

If you are **friendly with** someone you like each other and enjoy spending time together, as in:

> *She is friendly with several of the women who have children at her daughter's school.*

frightened of *see* afraid of

full of/filled with

If something is **full of** people or things it contains a very large number of them, sometimes to the extent that it can hardly contain any more, as in:

> *The bus was full of senior pupils from the nearby school.*

> *The cellar was full of rubbish.*

If something is **filled with** people or things it is **full of** them, as in:

> *She was trying to smile although her eyes were filled with tears.*

> *The hall was filled with people about an hour before the meeting was due to start.*

glad
glad about
If you are **glad about** something you are pleased and happy about it, as in:

> *We have discovered that we can get a flight from our local airport and we're very glad about that.*

glad for
If you are **glad for** someone you are pleased that they have got something or done something, as in:

> *Our son has got the job he applied for and we're so glad for him.*

glad of
If you are **glad of** something you are happy that you have it and you are grateful for it, as in:

> *He's had to work overtime a lot recently, but he was glad of the extra money so near to Christmas.*

glad to
If you are **glad to** do something you are willing and keen to do it, as in:

> *I'll be glad to look after the children for you this afternoon.*

graduate from
If you **graduate from** a university or college you get a degree from it, often a first degree, as in:

> *Many young people now have difficulty in getting jobs when they graduate from university.*

grateful

grateful for

If you are **grateful for** something you are happy to have it and feel that you want to thank someone for it, as in:

We are very grateful for all the donations to our charity.

grateful to

If you are **grateful to** someone for something you feel that you want to thank them for it, as in:

We are so grateful to everyone who has given us their support.

guilty

guilty about/feel guilty at

If you feel **guilty about** something you feel bad and ashamed because you know that you have done something bad or wrong, as in:

I feel guilty about forgetting your birthday.

The phrase **feel guilty at** means the same, as in:

They feel guilty at not inviting him to their party.

guilty of

If you are **guilty of** something you have done something bad, wrong or criminal, as in:

The jury found him guilty of manslaughter.

He's guilty of bullying the younger children.

in the habit of *see* **accustomed to**

half/half of

You can use either **half** or **half of** to refer to an amount that is one of two equal parts that make up a whole. You can use **half of** instead of **half** in front of a noun or noun group beginning with a determiner, although **half** is the more common, as in:

He has done half his work for today.

The child ate only half her lunch.

She has been in and out of hospital for half of her adult life.

Her father was overseas with the army for half of her childhood.

You use **half of** not **half** in front of pronouns, as in:

I haven't finished my essay but I've done half of it.

More than half of our foreign students went back to their own countries after graduating.

You use **half** not **half of** in front of words such as *hour, kilo, metre*, etc, as in:

It will take us half an hour to get there.

I need half a kilo of flour for this recipe.

harmful to

If something is **harmful to** someone or something it has a bad effect on them, as in:

Exhaust fumes from cars are harmful to the environment.

The substance does not seem to affect adults but it is harmful to young children.

hear of/hear about

If you **hear of** something you find out about it, as in:

She's heard of a job that would suit her very well.

You can also use **hear about** in this sense, as in:

We only heard about her promotion yesterday.

heard of

You can use **heard of** to show that you have knowledge about someone or something, as in:

Have you heard of a town called Seaway?

We thought we knew the area well, but we've never heard of a town called Seaway.

hope

hope for

You use **hope for** when you want something to happen and think that it is possible, as in:

She's hoping for some sunshine on her wedding day.

We're the better players and we're hoping for victory today.

hope of

If there is **hope of** something happening you want it to happen and think that it might, as in:

Doctors have hope of a cure in the near future.

Their army outnumbered ours and there was no hope of victory.

incapable of *see* capable of

incompatible with *see* compatible with

inferior to/superior to

If someone or something is said to be **inferior to** someone or something else, they are not as good or they are of poorer quality, as in:

You shouldn't feel inferior to them just because they have more money than you do.

This material is inferior to that one.

The opposite of this is **superior to**, as in:

> *The team that is playing this week is far superior to the one that played last week.*

inquire into

If you **inquire into** something you ask questions in order to get information about it, as in:

> *The police are inquiring into the company's profits because they suspect the owner of fraud.*

insist on

If you **insist on** doing something you say very firmly that you will do it, as in:

> *She insisted on getting a taxi to the airport although we offered to drive her there.*

intention of

If you say that you have every **intention of** doing something, you mean that you definitely plan to do it, as in:

> *He says that he has every intention of finishing his project today.*

If you say that you have no **intention of** doing something, you mean that you are definitely not going to do it, as in:

> *They say they've done nothing wrong and they have no intention of apologizing.*

interfere/meddle

interfere in

If you **interfere in** something you get involved in it and try to influence it or change it in some way although it's not really your business, and other people do not want you to get involved, as in:

> *The new owner promised that he would not interfere in the day-to-day running of the business.*

The expression **meddle in** means much the same, as in:

*The old lady resents the fact that her son tries to
meddle in her financial affairs.*

interfere with

If something **interferes with** something it prevents it from
happening successfully or as planned, as in:

*It looks as though the weather is going to interfere
with our planned barbecue.*

The bad weather interfered with their plans.

involved

involved in

If you are **involved in** something you take part in it, often very
actively, or are connected with it, as in:

Police suspect that he was involved in the robbery.

My son is very involved in sport at school.

involved with

If you are **involved with** something it means that you take part in
it, often very actively, as in:

She is involved with the local church.

If you are **involved with** someone it can mean that you are working
with them or spending time with them, or that you are connected
with them in some way, as in:

*They've been involved with each other in business
before.*

*He feels that he wants to be more involved with his
children.*

However, it can also mean that you are having a romantic
relationship with someone, as in:

We think she's involved with a man from her work.

irrespective of/regardless of

Irrespective of means 'having no effect on a situation' or 'having no importance or relevance', as in:

> *The competition is open to all local artists,*
> *irrespective of age.*

Irrespective of means much the same as **regardless of**, as in:

> *Our aim is for all students with suitable academic*
> *qualifications to get a university education,*
> *regardless of their financial situation.*

lack of

If there is a **lack of** something there is either not enough of it or a complete absence of it, as in:

> *Because of a lack of funds, we have no option but to*
> *close the youth club.*

lean on

Lean on has several meanings. Literally it means to rest on something or someone for support, as in:

> *She leant on her son's arm as they walked slowly*
> *up the road.*

Lean on can also mean to rely or depend on someone for support, as in:

> *She's a single mother with three young children*
> *and she leans quite heavily on her parents.*

Lean on also has a more sinister side and can mean to try to influence or persuade someone by threatening them in some way, as in:

> *The blackmailer leant even harder on his victim in*
> *the hope of getting more money.*

liable

liable for

If you are **liable for** something then you are legally responsible for something or for the cost of something, as in:

> *He doesn't earn enough to be liable for income tax.*

> *If you take the matter to court and lose you may be held liable for their costs as well as your own.*

liable to

If someone or something is **liable to** do something they are likely to do it, as in:

> *She is liable to lose her temper rather badly if anyone disagrees with her.*

> *The kitchen door is liable to slam shut if there's a wind blowing.*

If you are **liable to** something you are likely to be affected by it, as in:

> *He is liable to be a bit impulsive sometimes.*

limit to *see* **restrict to**

loyal to/disloyal to

If you are **loyal to** someone or something you are faithful to them and always give them your support, as in:

> *Some of the soldiers remained loyal to their leader after the mutiny.*

The opposite of **loyal to** is **disloyal to,** as in:

> *The soldier was accused of being disloyal to his regiment.*

masquerade as

If you **masquerade as** someone you pretend to be that person, as in:

> *The thief masqueraded as a security officer in order to gain admittance to the bank.*

meddle in *see* **interfere in**

meet with

If you **meet with** something it happens to you or you experience it, as in:

> *The climber met with a terrible accident and is badly injured.*

> *You can expect your wind farm proposal to meet with a lot of local opposition.*

There is a modern tendency, especially in business circles, to use **meet with** where **meet** is perfectly adequate, as in:

> *We plan to meet with their representatives next week.*

merge

merge into

If one thing **merges into** another the difference between them gradually fades and it's difficult to separate them, as in:

> *The grey clouds merged into the grey sea and it was difficult to see the horizon.*

merge with

If a firm should **merge with** another the two firms join together and form a single firm, as in:

> *Our small PR company is to merge with a large city firm.*

mindful of

If you are **mindful of** something you remember about it and take it into consideration when you do something, as in:

> *You must be mindful of your responsibilities as leader of a group of teenagers.*

> *Mindful of the dangers of sudden avalanches in the region, we decided to ski elsewhere.*

model on

If you **model** yourself **on** someone you try to act like them because you admire them and want to be like them, as in:

> *Many teenage girls try to model themselves on whatever female pop star is popular at the time.*

native to

If an animal or plant is **native to** somewhere, that is where it exists naturally and its natural habitat is there, as in:

> *These orchids are native to South America.*

> *The kangaroo is native to Australia.*

near to/close to

If something is **near to** something it is a very short distance away from it, as in:

> *Their house is quite near to the village.*

Near to can also be used to mean that someone or something is almost in a particular state, as in:

> *His wife was very near to giving birth when they arrived at the hospital.*

Close to can be used in both these meanings, as in:

> *Our new flat is close to the city centre.*

> *The firm is close to bankruptcy.*

See also **next to** on the following page.

need

in need of

If you are **in need of** something you require it or it is necessary that you have it, as in:

> *We are in need of extra funding to finish the project.*

need for

If there is a **need for** something it is necessary or must be done, as in:

> *There is an urgent need for fresh water in the refugee camp.*

> *There is no need for everyone to go.*

next to

If something is **next to** something it is physically by its side, as in:

> *The table was next to the bed.*

> *The houses were right next to each other.*

See also **near to** opposite.

object to

If you **object to** something, you do not approve of it or you do not agree with it, as in:

> *Local residents are sure to object to the new parking restrictions.*

A more formal way of saying this is **raise objections to**, as in:

> *They have not yet raised any objections to the proposed new scheme.*

oblivious of/to

Some people still object to the use of **oblivious to**, insisting that **oblivious of** is the only correct form. However, the use of **oblivious to** is increasing, partly because it is the preferred option in American English. It can no longer be regarded as wrong, although it still raises some objections.

Both **oblivious of** and **oblivious to** originally meant 'no longer aware of' or 'forgetful of', as in:

> *Longing for a swim after the long hot drive, and oblivious of the warning she had received about strong currents, she plunged into the waves.*

Now both expressions are often used to mean 'simply unaware of something', as in:

> *Oblivious to the passage of time, she suddenly*
> *realized that darkness had fallen and she was still*
> *far from home.*

obsessed by/with

If you are **obsessed by** someone or something you think or worry about them all the time, finding it difficult to think about anything else, as in:

> *She's totally obsessed by her appearance and*
> *spends most of her salary on cosmetics and designer*
> *clothes.*

You can also use **obsessed with** in the same way, as in:

> *He's obsessed with football and loves to watch his*
> *favourite team in action.*

opportunity for/to

If you have the **opportunity for** something it is possible for you to get it or achieve it, as in:

> *The company's owner saw the offer as an*
> *opportunity for expansion.*

> *The book group was an excellent opportunity for us*
> *all to meet old friends once a month.*

This can also be expressed using the **opportunity to** do something, as in:

> *It was a once-in-a-lifetime opportunity to travel to*
> *other parts of the world.*

opposite of

If something or someone is the **opposite of** something or someone else, they are completely different from each other in some way, as in:

> *She is quiet and studious, quite the opposite of her*
> *fun-loving sister.*

opposed to

If you are **opposed to** something then you strongly disapprove of it, as in:

> *Many of the town's residents are opposed to the idea*
> *of a new out-of-town supermarket and they are*
> *launching a campaign against it.*

opt for

If you **opt for** something you choose it rather than something else, as in:

> *She was offered a place at Oxford, but she's opted*
> *for a university nearer home.*

owing to *see* because of

pleased

pleased about

If you are **pleased about** something you are happy about it, as in:

> *Our daughter is getting married to a really nice*
> *man and my husband and I are very pleased about*
> *it.*

pleased with

If you are **pleased with** something you like it and are satisfied with it, as in:

> *She was very pleased with her Christmas present*
> *from her aunt.*

pleasure

take pleasure in

If you **take pleasure in** something you enjoy it, as in:

> *He took pleasure in watching golf on the TV.*

pore over

If you **pore over** something you look at it for a long time and read it carefully, as in:

> *Three of us pored over the map but we couldn't find the village we were looking for.*

prefer to

If you **prefer** something or someone **to** something or someone else, you like it better and would rather have it, as in:

> *I prefer country life to life in the city, but I have to live in the city for the sake of my work.*

preferable to

If something or someone is **preferable to** something or someone else they are considerably better, more suitable, etc, as in:

> *From a health point of view fresh fruit is preferable to sweet desserts.*

> *To me train travel is preferable to air travel.*

present at *see* absent from

prevent from

If something **prevents** you **from** doing something it stops you from doing it, as in:

> *Heavy traffic prevented us from getting there in time.*

prior to

Prior to is a formal way of saying 'before', as in:

> *Prior to his retirement he was chief executive of a large textile business.*

prohibit from

If something or someone **prohibits** you **from** doing something you are not allowed to do it, as in:

> *The new law prohibits people from smoking in here.*

Prohibit from is often used in the passive in formal contexts, as in:

> *Members of the public are prohibited from touching any of the museum exhibits.*

protest
protest against

If you **protest against** something you say that you strongly disagree with and disapprove of something, often saying so publicly in company with other people who have the same opinion, as in:

> *A large crowd gathered in the city's main square to protest against the proposed changes to the Human Rights Bill.*

protest at

If you **protest at** something, you say that you strongly disagree with and disapprove of something, as in:

> *Many people have protested at the government's handling of the economy.*

proud of

If you are **proud of** someone you think that they have done something good and you admire them, as in:

> *She is proud of her son for having done so well in his exams.*

If you are **proud of** something you are very pleased to have it or have done it, as in:

> *He's very proud of his new car and he polishes it every weekend.*

> *He's very proud of getting a place in the school football team.*

provide for

If you **provide for** someone you give them the things, such as food and clothing, that they need to live on, as in:

> *She works hard in order to be able to provide for*
> *her children.*

react to

If you **react to** something you behave in a particular way as a result of it, as in:

> *She reacted with great joy to the news that her*
> *daughter had given birth to a little girl.*

> *How do you think the stock market will react to the*
> *news that unemployment is rising?*

The noun from **react** is **reaction**. If you have a **reaction to** something it affects you in some way, as in:

> *She had a very bad reaction to the antibiotics*
> *which they gave her.*

recover from

If you **recover from** an illness or a bad or unpleasant situation you get well again or return to your previous state, as in:

> *She took a long time to recover from a nasty virus.*

> *Do you think the economy will ever recover*
> *completely from this recession?*

refer to

If you **refer to** someone or something you mention or speak about them, as in:

> *She's clearly very fond of her grandfather and*
> *constantly refers to him in her conversation with*
> *others.*

reflect on/upon

If you **reflect on** something you think about it very carefully and deeply, as in:

> *Unsure what to do after finishing school, he*
> *reflected on all his options.*

Reflect upon is a slightly more formal version of this.

refrain from

If you **refrain from** doing something you do not let yourself do it even though you may want to, as in:

> *Please refrain from eating or drinking in the library.*

> *For my wife's sake I refrained from telling my sister-in-law exactly what I thought of her behaviour.*

Refrain from is used in quite formal contexts.

regardless of *see* irrespective of

rely on/upon

If you **rely on** someone or something you need their support in order to survive, be successful, etc, as in:

> *She relied on her parents' generous financial support while she was a young actress struggling to get parts.*

> *The country can no longer rely on tourism alone to ensure its future.*

Rely upon is a slightly more formal version of this.

remind of

If someone or something **reminds** you **of** someone or something, they make you remember or think of that person or thing because they are similar in some way, as in:

> *She reminds me very much of her mother at that age, both in temperament and looks.*

renege on

If you **renege on** a promise or an agreement, you do not do what you promised or agreed to do, as in:

> *We had plans to work with a local company on building fishing boats, but they have reneged on the agreement and left us without a business partner.*

resistant to

If something is **resistant to** something it is not affected or damaged by it, as in:

> *Fortunately these trees seem to be resistant to the disease which is decimating some of our forests.*

> *We need to use a metal that is resistant to rust.*

responsible

responsible for

If you are **responsible for** doing something it is your job or duty to get it done and you may be blamed if something goes wrong, as in:

> *As the person responsible for company security, he may lose his job for allowing unauthorized visitors into the building.*

If you are **responsible for** someone it is your job to look after them or take care of them and you may be blamed if something goes wrong, as in:

> *Each nursery assistant is responsible for four children.*

Responsible for also means causing something, as in:

> *Smoking cigarettes is responsible for a lot of deaths from lung cancer.*

responsible to

If you are **responsible to** someone they have a more senior position than you in an organization and you report to them and may have to explain to them why you have acted in the way you did, as in:

> *Ms Morrison is the new head of the sales department and you are all responsible to her.*

restrict to/limit to

If you **restrict** the size, amount, extent, etc, of something **to** something, you do not allow anything larger, greater, etc, than that, as in:

We restrict the number of people allowed in the hall to 400.

Membership is restricted to people over 60.

He restricts the amount he eats each day, in an attempt to lose weight.

Limit to is also used in this way, as in:

They are going to limit the time each gym member can spend on the rowing machine to 20 minutes.

result
result from

If something **results from** something it is caused by that, as in:

Some of the damage results from the fire and some from the water used to put it out.

result in

If something **results in** something it causes that to happen, as in:

The building of the factory resulted in a great many new jobs for the people in the surrounding area.

retire from

If you **retire from** something you stop doing something, often because you have reached a particular age or because you are ill, as in:

He is nearly 70 and has decided that the time has come for him to retire from his post as chairman of the company.

He decided to retire from professional football after injuring his leg very badly in the cup final.

revert to

If you **revert to** something you start doing something again that you used to do in the past, as in:

After he came out of prison his behaviour improved
for a time but he has now reverted to his old
criminal ways.

When her divorce is finalized she intends to revert
to her maiden name.

rich in

If something is **rich in** something it contains a lot of it, as in:

They eat a diet that is rich in calcium.

The area is rich in history.

rob of

If you **rob** someone **of** something you steal something from someone or take something away from someone, as in:

The thieves robbed the old man of his life savings.

His injury on the track robbed the athlete of a gold medal.

satisfied with

If you are **satisfied with** something you are pleased with it and cannot find fault with it, as in:

I am quite satisfied with the new arrangements.

sceptical

If you are **sceptical about** something you have doubts about whether it is true or whether it is likely to happen, as in:

I am sceptical about her account of the accident
because she is the wife of one of the drivers.

He says that he is very sceptical about our chances
of winning.

Sceptical of means the same as **sceptical about**, as in:

We are sceptical of her claim that she is related to
the dead man.

Her parents are sceptical of her insistence that she studies every single day.

sensitive to

If you are **sensitive to** someone else's feelings, needs, etc, you are aware of them and are able to understand them, as in:

He is sensitive to the family's grief, especially since it is not long since his own father died.

If someone or something is **sensitive to** something they are easily affected or damaged by it, as in:

The child is very sensitive to heat and comes out in a rash if she gets too hot.

The student is very sensitive to any form of criticism and needs to learn not to over-react to constructive criticism.

separate from

If you **separate** something or someone **from** something or someone, you divide them into two parts or sections, as in:

The meringue recipe says that I must separate the egg whites from the egg yolks.

It was school policy to separate the girls from the boys for most sporting activities.

If something **separates** something **from** something else, it is between them so that they are not right next to each other, as in:

A large hedge separates our garden from out next-door neighbour's garden and gives us each some privacy.

share

share out

If you **share** something **out** you divide it between two or more people, as in:

The birthday cake was shared out amongst all the
guests at the party.

share with

If you **share** something **with** someone you have it or use it together
with another person or other people, as in:

He has to share a locker with one of the other
students as there are not enough lockers.

She shares a flat with three girls that she was at
school with.

sick of

If you are **sick of** someone or something they bore you or they
have been irritating you for some time and you are tired of them,
as in:

I think we're both sick of all the talent shows on TV.

My neighbour is always interrupting me when I'm
busy and I'm sick of it.

Sick of is used in informal contexts.

similar to/similarity between

If something is **similar to** something it is like that thing but not
the same as it, as in:

Their house is quite similar to ours.

If you want to use the noun **similarity** to convey the same idea it is
followed by **between**, as in:

There is a similarity between our houses.

Similarity can also be followed by **to**, as in:

In that photograph she has a striking similarity to
her grandmother.

smell of

If something **smells of** something it has the smell or odour of that
thing, as in:

The room smells of flowers fresh from the garden.

He smells of stale sweat. Someone should tell him to use a deodorant.

sorry
sorry about

If you are **sorry about** something, you feel sad and ashamed about it, as in:

I am sorry about my behaviour the other day.

You can also use **sorry for** in this context, as in:

She's sorry for being late, but the traffic was very heavy because of an accident on the motorway.

sorry for

If you are **sorry for** someone you feel pity or sympathy for them, as in:

She feels really sorry for homeless people and tries to help by working as a volunteer at the local homeless shelter.

See **sorry about** above.

strive for
If you **strive for** something you try very hard to get it, as in:

She strives for perfection, but is rarely successful.

subject to
Subject (with the stress on the first syllable) **to** has various meanings. If someone or something is **subject to** something bad or unpleasant, they are likely to be affected by it, as in:

Both brothers are subject to occasional epileptic fits.

They have just announced that most train schedules are subject to delay or cancellation because of the heavy snow.

If something is **subject to** something happening, it depends on that thing happening for it to take place, as in:

I have been informed that the construction of a new hotel on the outskirts of town is subject to planning permission.

If something is **subject to** a law, rule, etc, it must obey that law, rule, etc, as in:

Working conditions for part-time employees are now subject to new regulations.

Subject to can also be a verb which means 'to make someone experience something unpleasant', as in:

We were subjected to noise night and day from the building site next to our hotel.

In the case of the verb **to subject**, the stress is on the second syllable.

substitute for
If something is a **substitute for** something else it is used instead of it, as in:

She uses an artificial sweetener as a substitute for sugar as part of her weight-loss plan.

If someone is a **substitute for** someone else they do the job that that person usually does, as in:

He is playing today as a substitute for the injured goalkeeper.

succeed in
If you **succeed in** doing something, you do or achieve what you set out to do, as in:

He succeeded in passing all his exams.

suffer from
If you **suffer from** something you are usually affected by something unpleasant such as disease, pain, etc, as in:

*She has been in a serious road accident and is
suffering from internal injuries.*

*The country is still suffering from the effects of the
recession.*

superior to *see* **inferior to**

susceptible to

If you are **susceptible to** something you are very likely to be
affected or influenced by it, as in:

These plants are particularly susceptible to disease.

The child is susceptible to chest infections.

suspicious of

If you are **suspicious of** someone, you do not trust them and think
that they may have done something wrong, as in:

*Anne's new boyfriend never says much about
himself and I'm rather suspicious of him.*

If you are **suspicious of** something you think that it may be
dishonest, illegal, etc, although you do not have any proof, as in:

*The policeman was suspicious of the car driver's
explanation and he wondered if the car was a
stolen car.*

sympathize with

If you **sympathize with** someone you feel sorry for them and
understand the problems they have, as in:

*I can sympathize with the people looking for work
because I've been unemployed several times in my
life.*

tamper with

If you **tamper with** something you make changes to it without
being asked to, often with the intention of deliberately damaging
it, as in:

His rival tampered with his car engine and caused him to crash.

tendency to

If someone or something has a **tendency to** do something they are likely to do it, as in:

Because of the increase in unemployment in the country people now have a tendency to stay in the jobs they have, rather than try to move on.

She has a tendency to get hyperactive after eating sweets.

think

think over

If you **think** something **over** you consider it very carefully before reaching a decision, as in:

They have offered him the job, but he has asked for some time to think it over before he decides whether to accept their offer or not.

think through

If you **think** something **through** you think about a possible course of action very carefully, considering all the things that might happen, as in:

I wasn't surprised their plan failed, because it was obvious that they simply hadn't thought it through.

think up

If you **think** something **up** you create it in your mind, often something inventive or imaginative, as in:

One of the prisoners of war thought up a clever escape plan that proved successful.

together with

Together with can mean in addition to something else, as in:

You need to produce your passport together with your birth certificate.

Together with can also be used to refer to someone who is also involved in something, as in:

Jim, together with Tom, climbed to the very summit of the mountain.

true to

If you are **true to** someone or something you remain loyal to them and continue to give them your support, whatever happens, as in:

Even after several serious defeats on the battlefield the troops remained true to their leader.

If you are **true to** your word or promise, you act or behave as you promised to do, as in:

She was true to her word and repaid the money I lent her by the end of the month.

unaware of *see* **aware of**

unconscious of *see* **aware of**

used to *see* **accustomed to**

wait

wait for

If you **wait for** someone or something you stay where you are until they arrive, as in:

I'm outside the cinema waiting for my son, but he's a bit late.

We're waiting for the bus.

If you **wait for** something to happen you are expecting it to happen, as in:

He is waiting for a flat to become vacant.

See **wait on** below.

wait on

If you **wait on** someone you bring food and drink to them at their table, especially in a restaurant, as in:

> *The young woman who waited on us in the*
> *restaurant was very polite.*

Wait on is sometimes used to mean 'to look after someone's needs', as in:

> *My aunt has come to visit us and she expects us all*
> *to wait on her, even though we are all very busy.*

Wait on is also used informally in British English to mean **wait for**, as in:

> *We are waiting on Jack to finish work.*

Many people disapprove of this last use and it should not be used in formal contexts.

5

PHRASAL VERBS

Prepositions can also cause problems when they are part of phrasal verbs but they are not the only culprits in this respect. A phrasal verb is a verb which can be combined with an adverb, with a preposition or with an adverb plus a preposition.

Examples of sentences containing the verb + adverb combination include:

*When the policeman saw the thief he **ran away**.*

*She felt dizzy and suddenly **fell down**.*

Examples of sentences containing the verb + preposition combination include:

*The children **ran through** the dark wood as fast as they could.*

*He **dived into** the deepest part of the pool.*

Examples of sentences containing the verb + adverb + preposition combination include:

*The party's tonight and I've decided to **go along with** Sue.*

*Mark's **gone off with** Jane on a camping holiday.*

Many features of English cause problems to both native speakers of English and learners of the language as a second or foreign language. However, this is not the case with phrasal verbs. Learners of English find these much more problematic than native speakers do.

Why should this be? Well, there is an element of intuition about language as far as your native language is concerned, and some of what a native speaker knows about phrasal verbs might be put down to that. Then there is the fact that the native speaker, to a large extent, automatically learns how to use language from listening to other people speaking, and later from reading. Somewhere along the way to school and during the educational process something will have been learnt about phrasal verbs.

Of course young native speakers may be completely unaware that they have this knowledge about the use of phrasal verbs. That is because they probably have no idea what a phrasal verb is. It is not a subject that crops up very often in the English language classes of native speakers. Quite a few of you who are currently reading this may be completely in the dark about the subject.

So what is a phrasal verb? Native speakers might not want to know. Perhaps they would rather ignore problems that they have so far not given a thought to because they have simply been doing what comes naturally. Meanwhile learners of English will most likely groan. Phrasal verbs to them are well-known troublemakers.

There are native speakers who feel passionately about the English language. Many of them do not like change and they want to preserve the language as it is. Unfortunately for them, language does not work like that. Society changes and language has to reflect these changes.

PHRASAL OR SINGLE VERB?

Some of the language preservationists dislike the growing tendency to use a phrasal verb where a single verb will do. For example, for a long time people were content to use the verb **meet** on its own. This was true of informal contexts, as in:

I'm meeting Rebecca for lunch tomorrow.

But it was also true of more formal contexts, as in:

The board of directors plan to meet their
management staff next week.

In recent years, however, people have begun to use the phrasal verb **meet with** instead of just the verb **meet** informally as with

*I'm **meeting with** Rebecca for lunch tomorrow.*

and more especially in formal contexts

*The board of directors plan to **meet with** their management staff next week.*

British English has acquired this habit from American English and objectors to it say that the use of **meet with** is completely unnecessary and pretentious. Nevertheless, the verb **meet with** seems to be here to stay, at least in formal contexts.

This use is also spreading to other verbs. For example, some people are no longer content to **consult** a professional about something. They prefer to **consult with** a professional, as in:

*He thinks that he has been dismissed unfairly and he has been advised to **consult with** his lawyer.*

Again, objections have been raised to this, on the same grounds as those to **meet with**, but they will not do any good. Trying to hold back changes to the language is a complete waste of time. Whatever anyone does, such changes will happen.

FIGURATIVE OR LITERAL MEANING?

One of the difficulties with phrasal verbs is that they frequently do not mean what they seem to be saying. You can know perfectly well the meaning of the individual words that make up the phrase, and yet be unable to understand the meaning of the phrase. As is the case with many idioms, many phrasal verbs are used figuratively and it is often not easy to deduce this figurative meaning from the literal meaning of the words making up the phrase.

Some figurative meanings of phrasal verbs are more difficult to deduce than others. Some are quite easy.

For example, in the sentence

The children will come through that door very soon.

the phrasal verb **come through** means just what it says, that the children will exit from the door soon.

However, in the sentence

*It was a miracle that so many soldiers came
through the war alive.*

the phrasal verb **came through** is not used exactly literally in
that sentence, but is used in a way that is only a short step from
the literal meaning. The sentence is referring to soldiers who
survived a war.

The sentence

*He got over the fence with difficulty and hoped
there were no guard dogs around.*

obviously refers to someone literally climbing over a fence to get
to the other side.

The sentence

*He never got over his fiancée's death and remained
unmarried all his life.*

refers to someone who has never recovered from something bad
that has happened. Again, the phrasal verb is not being used
exactly literally, but it is close enough to the literal meaning to be
easily deducible in context.

There are a great many examples of phrasal verbs of this
kind – not quite literal in meaning but fairly easy to understand
in context. Some are a step forward in difficulty from the
two phrasal verbs mentioned above, but still relatively easily
deducible, and they certainly do not usually cause any problems
to native speakers.

These include **look down on** and **look up to**. The phrase **look
down** means that you literally lower your eyes in order to see what
is below you. Similarly, the phrase **look up** means that you literally
raise your eyes in order to see what is above you.

There is a bit more to their literal meanings when you add the
prepositions **on** and **to** respectively. The phrasal verb **look down
on** means that you think that someone is much less important
than you are and so is inferior to you, as in:

*She looks down on students whose fathers work in
the local factory.*

The phrasal verb **look up to** means that you respect and admire someone as though they were much more important or better than you, as in:

> *He is a well-known artist as well as being a teacher and many of the students look up to him.*

The phrasal verb **look forward** means literally that you are looking at what is straight in front of you. If you add **to** *to* the phrase, as in **look forward to**, you are pleased or excited about something that you expect to happen sometime soon, as in:

> *The little girl is really looking forward to her friend's birthday party.*

The literal meaning of the phrasal verb **look through** should present no difficulties, as in:

> *We looked through the window at the rain.*

While its figurative meaning as applied to newspapers, reports, etc, is fairly obvious from the context, as in:

> *I have to look through the report before the meeting.*

When used of something that is done to people, however, things become more complicated. If you **look through** someone you look at them as though you have not noticed them, often because you are deliberately ignoring them because you are angry with them, as in:

> *As she came towards me I was about to speak to her but she looked right through me and walked on.*

Learners can be easily confused when the meaning of a phrasal verb seems quite easy to understand and then turns out not be. There may be an unexpected overtone or nuance that changes the meaning quite considerably. Take the sentence which was mentioned on page 121 as an example of a phrasal verb:

> *Mark's gone off with Jane on a camping holiday.*

Now we know nothing whatsoever about Mark and Jane or their relationship, and we do not need to know. All we are told is that they have gone on a camping holiday together.

On the other hand, if the sentence is

*Mark's **gone off with** Jim's wife.*

then we have grounds for some suspicion, and if the sentence then becomes

*Mark's **run off with** Jim's wife.*

then our suspicion appears to be well-founded. It would seem that Mark and Jim's wife have been having a relationship and they have decided to live together. It is amazing what you can learn from a little phrasal verb!

POSITION OF THE OBJECT

There is another problem that crops up with reference to phrasal verbs. Some phrasal verbs are intransitive and so do not take an object. Many of them, however, are transitive and do take an object. Therein lies the problem.

There is some variation in the position of this object. If the object is a noun or a short noun phrase it can sometimes be placed after the second word of the phrasal verb, as in:

*She is putting away the **dishes** in the cupboard.*

*The boxer knocked out his **opponent** in the first round.*

On the other hand, the noun or short noun phrase can sometimes be placed after the first word and before the second word of the phrasal verb, as in:

*The mayor is handing **trophies** over to the winners now.*

*She is putting the **dishes** away in the cupboard.*

In all the relevant sentences the object is in bold.

How do you decide where to put the noun or noun phrase? It is often a matter of taste or a matter of which form you think sounds better. Sometimes which sounds best depends on the length of the noun phrase.

When the object is a pronoun it usually precedes the second word of the phrasal verb, as in:

> *The ornament was broken into many pieces when the child knocked **it** over.*

> *The left-over food will taste all right if you warm **it** up.*

COMPLEX PHRASAL VERBS

A small selection follows of fairly complex phrasal verbs which have been formed from common verbs. There are many, many more, but this selection will show you phrasal verbs in action, so to speak. Most of these phrasal verbs have meanings which are more than just the sum of their parts. In other words, you cannot deduce their overall meaning just from knowing the meaning of the individual words. They are thus likely to be useful to native speakers of English as well as to learners.

PHRASAL VERBS IN ACTION

come
come down on

If you **come down on** someone or something you criticize or punish them for something they have done, as in:

> *The new head teacher said that she will come down heavily on bullies.*

come down with

If you **come down with** a disease or an infection you develop or begin to have it, as in:

> *I feel as though I am coming down with flu.*

come up with

If you **come up with** an idea, plan, etc, you think of it, often having thought about it for a considerable time, as in:

*They have finally come up with sufficient funding
to pay for the project.*

cut
cut back on

If you **cut back on** something you reduce the extent of it, often because you cannot afford to spend so much money on it, as in:

*The government are planning to cut back on
defence expenditure.*

cut down on

If you **cut down on** something you try to reduce the amount of it that you use or to reduce the number of times you do it, as in:

*She hasn't give up smoking although she's cut down
on the number of cigarettes she gets through in a
week.*

do
do away with

If you **do away with** something you get rid of it or abandon it, as in:

*They've introduced computerization and done
away with old-fashioned production methods.*

*The school did away with school uniform but
brought it back again a few years later.*

Do away with can also be used informally to mean 'to kill someone', as in:

*She looked so angry that I thought she was going to
do away with me!*

*The gang leader disappeared over a year ago, and
police think that members of a rival gang may have
done away with him.*

do out of

If you **do** someone **out of** something you stop them getting it or having it, sometimes dishonestly, as in:

*The workers went on strike because they said that
their employers had done them out of a bonus.*

*The schoolchildren felt that they had been done out
of a day's holiday.*

get
get along with
If you **get along with** someone you find it easy to be with them and
to enjoy their company, as in:

*Jill's boyfriend doesn't get along very well with her
family.*

*It's good that all the members of the team get along
so well with each other.*

get away with
If you **get away with** something you are not punished or scolded
for doing it, as in:

*He gets away with being really naughty when he
stays with his grandparents.*

get behind with
If you **get behind with** something you are late or slow in doing it,
and have not made as much progress as you should have done,
as in:

*The landlord is angry because we're getting behind
with the rent again.*

*I'm going to work late at the office this evening as
I'm getting behind with my paperwork.*

get down to
If you **get down to** something you start doing it seriously and
paying a lot of attention to it, as in:

*I'm going to get down to some revision right away
as I have a big test tomorrow.*

> *We really must get down to thinking of ways to save money.*

get out of

If you **get out of** something you avoid doing something which you do not want to do, as in:

> *She's offered to do the shopping to get out of helping with the housework.*

> *He's been asked to speak at the meeting but he's trying desperately to get out of it.*

get round to

If you **get round to** doing something you do something that you have been intending to do for some time, or that you should have done before, but have been too busy or unwilling to do, as in:

> *It was the day before Christmas Eve before I finally got round to writing some Christmas cards.*

> *He asked her to marry him several months ago, but he hasn't got round to buying her an engagement ring yet.*

get through to

If you **get through to** someone by telephone you are able to contact them and speak to them, as in:

> *Telephone reception isn't very good in that part of the world and I wasn't able to get through to my sister.*

> *The line was engaged at first but I soon got through to the hospital.*

However, you do not need always need a telephone in order to **get through to** someone. The phrase can also mean 'to succeed in getting someone to understand something, although this may be difficult', as in:

> *He didn't seem to understand how dangerous the*

*situation was, but I finally got through to him before
it was too late.*

*Please can someone get through to the students that
these exams are important and they must get some
studying done.*

get up to

If you **get up to** something you do something bad or naughty, as
in:

*Those kids are giggling behind the shed and I'm
sure they're getting up to mischief.*

*The police were sure that the youths standing on the
street corner were planning to get up to something,
but they didn't know what.*

Get up to is used in informal contexts.

go

go along with

If you literally **go along with** someone you go with them to
somewhere, as in:

*She wants me to go along to the party with her, but
I'm not in the mood.*

*I went along to the opening ceremony with my
parents.*

If you **go along with** a ruling, decision, etc, you accept it and obey
it, as in:

*Although he could have appealed against the
court's ruling he decided to go along with it.*

If you **go along with** someone or with their idea, policy etc, you
accept it or agree with it, as in:

*Most of the teachers go along with the head's
proposals for changes to the school timetable.*

go back on

If you **go back on** something, you do not do what you promised or agreed to do, as in:

> *She's not very trustworthy so I'm not really surprised that she's gone back on her promise to help.*

go in for

If you **go in for** a competition of some kind you take part in it, as in:

> *I don't think he's fit enough to go in for the marathon race.*

> *They're both going in for the tennis club tournament.*

If you **go in for** a particular kind of work you make it your job or career, as in:

> *She wanted to go in for medicine but her exam results were not good enough.*

> *His father wants him to go in for accountancy.*

go in with

If you **go in with** someone you decide to become their business partner, as in:

> *John's started a gardening business and Jack's decided to go in with him.*

go off

If someone **goes off** someone or something it means they cease to like them or it, as in:

> *My sister has gone off her best friend since they quarrelled.*

go off with

If someone **goes off with** something they take something that belongs to someone else, usually without permission, as in:

> *I showed him rather a valuable book and I later*
> *discovered that he had gone off with it.*

go through with

If you **go through with** something you continue doing it until it has been completed or achieved, as in:

> *He had threatened to quit university several times*
> *before, but none of his friends thought he would*
> *ever go through with it.*

> *The government's proposal to raise taxes was so*
> *unpopular that they did not go through with the*
> *scheme.*

hold

hold out for

If you **hold out for** someone or something you insist on waiting for what you want and refuse to accept anything less, as in:

> *She said she was holding out for a tall, dark,*
> *handsome, wealthy man.*

> *He turned down several jobs after graduation*
> *because he said he was*
> *holding out for something interesting*
> *and well-paid.*

hold out on

If you **hold out on** someone you refuse to tell them something or to give them something that they want, as in:

> *He assured the police that he had no idea where his*
> *friend was but they were sure he was holding out*
> *on them.*

The phrasal verb **hold out on** is usually used in an informal context.

keep

keep in with

If you **keep in with** someone you remain friendly with them, usually because this may help you to get something you want, as in:

> *She only keeps in with Jim because he's got a car and gives her a lift to and from work every day.*

> *There's a rumour that Anne's going to be made head of department and everyone's keeping in with her as a result.*

keep on at

If you **keep on at** someone you repeatedly ask or tell them something so that they get annoyed or upset, as in:

> *Her father kept on at her about working harder at school until she lost her temper and stormed out of the house.*

> *The boy kept on at his mother about getting a mobile phone and fed up with his nagging she eventually agreed.*

keep out of

If you **keep out of** something you avoid being involved in an unpleasant or difficult situation, as in:

> *If the two sisters start arguing with each other, keep out of it or they'll both turn against you.*

> *If the boy doesn't keep out of trouble for the rest of the term he'll be asked to leave.*

keep up with

If you **keep up with** someone you stay in contact with them, as in:

> *Over the years she's kept up with one or two of her school friends and they like to meet for coffee occasionally.*

> *We promised to keep up with each other after we left university, but we've lost contact.*

make

make off with/make away with

If you **make off with** something you steal something and take it away, as in:

> *He had foolishly left the keys in the ignition and a thief made off with his car.*

> *The dog leapt onto the table and made off with the remains of the roast beef.*

Make away with means the same as **make off with**, as in:

> *Someone's made away with my wallet.*

make up to

If you **make up to** someone you flatter them and say pleasant things to them so that they will give you something, or do something, that you want, as in:

> *She's usually horrible to her brother, but she's making up to him tonight because she wants to borrow his car.*

> *The politician is going round the town making up to everyone he meets because he wants their vote at the next election.*

make up for

If you **make up for** something you do something that tries to put right a bad situation, as in:

> *He bought his mother a beautiful, expensive new vase to make up for breaking her favourite one.*

> *Her father promised to take her to see a film during the week to make up for having to cancel their trip to the cinema at the weekend.*

pull out of

If you **pull out of** something you get out of a difficult or dangerous situation, as in:

We're pulling out of the market because it's no longer profitable.

The territory is too dangerous and our army is pulling out.

put
put down to

If you **put** something **down to** something you think or say that something is caused by something, as in:

She put her good mood down to the lovely weather.

The firm put the slump in their profits down to the recession.

put in for

If you **put in for** something you apply for it, as in:

There's a more senior job coming up soon and I'm putting in for it.

She's putting in for extended maternity leave.

put up to

If you **put** someone **up to** something you encourage them to do something foolish, dangerous or wrong, as in:

Her friends put her up to stealing a packet of sweets from the shop.

His brother put him up to climbing on the roof and he fell off.

put up with

If you **put up with** something or someone you accept an unpleasant situation or person without complaining or tolerate someone or something, as in:

She said that she had put up with her unreasonable boss as long as she could.

> *They moved house because they couldn't put up
> with their noisy neighbours any longer.*

stand
stand out against
If you **stand out against** something you go on strongly opposing it, as in:

> *The other political parties are standing out against
> the spending cuts proposed by the government.*

stand out for
See **hold out for** under **hold** on page 133.

stand up for
If you **stand up for** someone or something you defend or support them when they are under an attack of some kind, as in:

> *The new regime is very harsh and we all need to
> stand up for our basic human rights.*

> *Weaker, younger pupils who cannot stand up for
> themselves are protected from bullying by older,
> stronger pupils.*

stand up to
If you **stand up to** someone you refuse to be bullied by them and are able to resist their attacks or demands, as in:

> *He did his best to stand up to the bully but it was
> not easy.*

> *Although it is a small country, its inhabitants stand
> up to the continual attacks of its powerful neighbour.*

take
take up on
If you **take** someone **up on** something you accept an offer or a suggestion that they have made to you, as in:

> *I'll take you up on your offer of a lift home, if that's
> all right?*

*I'm busy tonight but I'll take you up on your
suggestion of dinner some time soon.*

take up with

If you **take up with** someone you start being friendly with them
and spending quite a lot of time with them, or you start a romantic
relationship with them, as in:

*Their son's taken up with some kids that have been
in trouble with the police.*

*We hear that Kate's taken up with a boy in her
class.*

walk

walk away from

If you literally **walk away from** someone or something you just
move away from them by walking. If you figuratively **walk away
from** a situation you do not try to deal with it but leave it or ignore
it, as in:

*Her wealthy brother could have helped her with
her failing business, but he chose to walk away
from it all and left her to cope alone.*

*After their last quarrel he felt that their friendship
was at an end and the time had come to walk away
from it.*

walk in on

If you **walk in on** someone you enter somewhere unexpectedly
and see them, or several people, doing something private or
secret which may embarrass you or them, as in:

I walked in on my aunt when she was in the shower.

*She walked in on her parents when they were in a
passionate embrace.*

walk off with

If you **walk off with** something you win something, such as a
trophy, very easily, as in:

*There was no one in the tournament who was
anywhere near her standard and she walked off
with the championship trophy.*

*They were easily the most talented pop group in the
competition and walked off with first prize.*

6

DISPOSING OF DISCRIMINATION

DESEXING THE LANGUAGE

There are various reasons for language change. A major influence on the English language was the escalation, from the 1960s on, of a movement which was not primarily aimed at language, but which was to give rise to enormous changes in it. This was the women's movement, and its purpose was to improve the social and economic status of women in society, and give women the same rights as men.

Some progress had been made when women in Britain had finally been allowed to vote in elections to parliament after a hard-fought campaign by the suffragettes, but that was only the first step. During the two World Wars, especially the second of these, many women had worked outside the home for the first time. In many cases they were doing jobs, such as driving ambulances and working in factories, that men had formerly done.

When these men came back from the war they found that their women had tasted independence and did not want to return to the kitchen and the nursery for the rest of their lives. They wanted to work outside the home and, in time, they wanted the same rate of pay and the same employment rights as men doing the same job.

FEMINIST ADDITIONS TO THE LANGUAGE

It was a long and slow process, and the fight is not over yet. Some people feel there is still a so-called **glass ceiling**, a term used to describe the invisible barrier that prevents women from achieving their full, senior potential in the workplace. **Glass ceiling** was one of the additions to the English language that the battle for equal rights for women brought with it, and there were others.

Before the fight for equality there was a distinct male bias in the English language. If the sex of a person was not known, or not given, the person was assumed to be male. As women gained equality in society, calls were made for changes to the language to rectify this male bias and some changes have occurred.

As well as **glass ceiling**, the language additions brought us **male chauvinist**, used to describe a man who is convinced of the inferiority of women and who is totally opposed to the idea of equal rights for women. Men who were particularly opposed to the idea and acted accordingly were described as **male chauvinist pigs**. It is odd how the poor pig seems to get an unfair deal in language!

Of course, the struggle for equality brought us **sex discrimination** and **sexism** – the unfair treatment of people on account of their gender. On the positive side, the fight for equal rights for women and for other people who were discriminated against (of which more later) brought us not only **equal opportunity**, but also **positive discrimination** and **affirmative action**.

The term **positive discrimination** was coined to describe the practice of giving a particular number of jobs, university places, etc, to people who were in the habit of being treated unfairly because of their gender, race, etc. **Positive discrimination** was the phrase favoured by the British. The American equivalent was **affirmative action**. Both expressions proved quite durable. I am not so sure about the actions that they described.

REMOVING –MAN

The contribution to the language made by the battle for women's rights was not just about additions to the vocabulary. The existing language was itself found to be just as sexist as many employers.

Many compound nouns indicating some kind of job or position ended in **–man**, even though this job or position might easily be held by a woman. **Fireman** and **policeman** are cases in point, and they became **fire fighter** and **police officer** when **sexism** was removed. **Foreman** became **supervisor** or something similar. So far so good. These words managed to bring off a relatively smooth transition.

The word **chairman** was not so lucky. Because it ended in **–man** it had to go, but what would it become? That was a difficult question and it was given some tricky answers. Part of the trouble was that there had always been a lot of female **chairmen** around. Not many of them had succeeded in smashing through the glass ceiling to become heads of companies, but many of them had been designated chairmen of societies and social organizations.

Younger women in particular wanted to get shot of the **–man** element at all costs. A reasonably popular replacement choice was **–person**, but it was far from popular with everyone. Many people absolutely hated **chairperson** and said so. Bear in mind that, although there is always a degree of language change going on, the scale and the speed of change was not as great when **chairman** was trying to divest itself of its obvious masculinity. Many women, especially older women, said that, given the choice, they would rather be a **chairman** than a **chairperson** any day.

One proposed alternative was **chair**. This also brought forth much protest. I heard one rather matronly woman declaim that she had no intention of becoming something neuter like a chair. She would rather be a chairman.

Somehow the whole thing has calmed down, as things do in time. I do not think that there has ever been an across-the-board solution. Some people chairing a meeting or a social organization will be chairs and some will be chairpersons. Probably, some, whatever their gender, may still be chairmen.

Of course the use of **–man** in compound nouns was not restricted to its association with **chair**. There were other words that fell into this category, words such as **barman** and **spokesman**, for example. A different fate has befallen these two. Although attempts have been made to impose **barperson** on pub-goers they have not been all that successful. **Barman** is still flourishing. More surprisingly, so is **barmaid**, which you would think would be regarded as sexist in the extreme. It has fought off not only **barperson**, but other attempts to replace it with words such as **bar assistant** and **bar attendant**.

Spokesman, however, has not shown the same capacity for survival as **barmaid**. **Spokesperson** is one of a few **–person** words that do not automatically reduce people to fits of laughter. The word has become quite common when the gender of the person speaking on behalf of an organization is not known. Obviously, if the gender of that person is known then the correct gender can be assigned and we could end up with a **spokesman** or a **spokeswoman**. This should be acceptable to all although that is not always the case. It is no surprise that many organizations tend to duck this issue and go for the word **representative** instead.

The proposed substitution of **person** for **man** was considered by many, at least at first, to be hilarious. As a result it gave rise to a great deal of exaggeration and satire. People would find amusement in substituting **person** for **man** in words such as **manhole**. Others with no thought of humour attempted to get rid of the word **manhole** by substituting **sewer access hole** or **utility access hole**. Fortunately most of us do not have much call to refer to manholes, unless we trip over one or, worse, fall down one. In such cases we are probably not overly concerned with what they are called.

IS MANKIND NO MORE?

We are not yet finished with the word **man**. **Man** was also formerly used universally to refer to human beings as a group or to human beings from a particular period of history, as in:

Man has destroyed the habitats of many animals.

Early man lived in caves and wore animal skins.

Sometimes **man** in this sense was spelt with a capital letter, sometimes not, but it was not the spelling that caused the problem. It was the fact that its use ignored half the human race, the women.

Some people continue to use **man** in this sense as though it were a generic word referring to any human being rather than to a member of the male sex. If you want to avoid this use you can often substitute **humans** or **human beings** or **the human race**, whichever seems the most appropriate in the context. Similarly, **mankind** can be avoided by the use of **humankind**, but do avoid using **personkind** or you will run the risk of being greeted by the same kind of hilarity that **personhole** gives rise to.

PERSON

The word **person** may often be used satirically when it is used as part of a compound word such as **personhole**, but it is a perfectly respectable word when used on its own. It plays a useful part in avoiding male bias in language. Formerly, someone seeking a new employee would very probably have spoken or written of the need to find 'the right man for the job'. Nowadays the would-be employer would be much more likely to say or write 'the right person for the job'. When more than one person is involved **people** should be used instead of **men**.

–ESS

The suffix **–ess** may not look like a particularly troublesome word but its appearance is deceptive. It has played a major part in the fight for equality of the sexes.

Formerly, some words, such as **author, poet, sculptor**, whose gender is not obvious, unless the identity of the individual person is known, were automatically assumed to be masculine and they had feminine forms, **authoress, poetess** and **sculptress**. The call to stamp out sexism from language meant that these **–ess** forms were considered belittling to women and so were found to be unacceptable.

The **–ess** was thus removed from these and some other words and they became the gender-free or neutral words, **author, poet** and **sculptor**. However, the English language is not always consistent – far from it. So we find that some feminine forms, such as **waitress**, are still in common use, while both **actor** and **actress** are commonly used for a female actor.

Manageress is still sometimes used to refer to a woman who is in charge of a shop, but not to a woman who has climbed the company executive ladder to managerial level. The job of **air hostess**, once thought to be ultra-glamorous, is now known by the more mundane term of **flight attendant**, whether the person doing the job is a man or a woman.

Alternatives to **–ess** such as **–trix** are also disappearing. As is the case with **–ess**, the former male term is now seen as the neutral term and the word **proprietor** can refer either to a male or female owner of a business.

–ETTE

If **–ess** was often, by this time, considered to be something of a despised suffix, how much more despised was the suffix **–ette**. It was belittling on two counts. Like **–ess**, it was used to form a female equivalent of a male word, but it was also used to refer to a diminutive or small form.

Fortunately, there were never that many **–ette** words referring to women around. Probably the best known was **usherette**, a woman who showed you to your seat in a cinema or theatre. Nowadays, places which still have people showing patrons to their seats would probably refer to the male or female person doing the job as an **usher**.

Female jockeys were sometimes called **jockettes** but, although there have long been a large number of female riders around, women jockeys have been few on the ground. The word **jockette** never really caught on before it was ruled out of order.

The word **hackette** was, and is still, occasionally used to refer to a female journalist. Its use is usually satirical and women journalists sometimes use it humorously of themselves.

LADY/WOMAN/FEMALE

We are not yet finished with the influence of women on language, but this next issue has nothing to do with men. It is purely a female issue and one that sounds as though it belongs more to class than gender. It concerns the use of the words **lady** and **woman**.

Formerly the word **lady** was often used instead of **woman** because doing so was thought to be part of the code of polite behaviour. Many parents still encourage their children to refer to a woman as a lady. For example, a mother might say to her young child in a bus:

> *'Sue, come and sit on my knee and give that lady your seat.'*

Some older people might feel uncomfortable about using the word **woman** since they will have been taught not to do so. However, for the most part **woman** is now the accepted term and **lady** can be regarded as rather a condescending term. Thus

cleaning lady is to be avoided and there is no need to use **cleaning woman** since **cleaner** will be absolutely fine. After all the person doing the cleaning might be a man!

There are some employment words which, even before the sexual revolution, could refer to either men or women, although there were far more men than women in the roles. Such words include **doctor** and **engineer**.

The term **lady doctor** was formerly quite commonly used to refer to a doctor who was a woman. This term is now old-fashioned and people who feel the need of consulting a doctor who is not a man probably quite happily refer to a **woman doctor**. Alternatively, it is perfectly all right to refer to a **female doctor**.

People are not so likely to have to worry about the gender of an engineer. Formerly it was not a problem at all because there were very few female engineers, engineering not being considered a suitable career for a woman. Now engineers who are female can follow the example set by doctors and be referred to as a **woman engineer** or a **female engineer**. This will also apply to various other trades, professions, etc, as in:

> *The company now employs quite a few female bus drivers.*

A similar problem can affect men if they take up a profession that was formerly restricted to women. For example, there are now more men taking up primary teaching but that has no linguistic problems. Like women, they are just teachers. But the same is not true of nurses. Formerly nurses were assumed to be women so when men started to take up nursing as a profession they became known as **male nurses**.

FEMALE AS A NOUN

As we have seen, **female** is perfectly acceptable as an adjective, but care must be taken if you are thinking of using it as a noun. It is fine to use it if you wish to refer to young people of the female sex who are too young to be described as women, as in:

> *He is the only man in a house full of females – his wife, his mother and his three young daughters.*

It can also be used to contrast with **male**, as in:

> *There are now twice the number of females as there*
> *are males in the club.*

It can be used of female animals without any protest.

However, the use of **female** as a noun can be regarded as disrespectful or insulting, as in:

> *Some interfering female has just told us that we*
> *can't park here.*

> *Who is the female wearing that dreadful hat?*

GIRL

Girl is obviously quite acceptable if it is used to refer to someone of the female sex who is either a child or an adolescent, as in:

> *The girls in the class have done better in the exam*
> *than the boys.*

When it is used of older people who are, in fact, women, the word **girl** can sometimes be regarded as patronizing or disrespectful when it is used by men. This is quite ironic as some men, particularly older men, think that they are being complimentary or courteous when using **girl** to refer to a woman who is quite obviously no longer as young as a girl, as in:

> *What would you girls like to drink?*

The 'stamping out of sexism' campaign may well have passed such men by.

It seems a bit unfair but it is quite all right for women who are no longer young to refer to their friends of a similar age as **girls**, as in:

> *My mother says she can't come to dinner tomorrow*
> *night as she always has a night out with the girls on*
> *a Thursday.*

SIGNIFICANT OTHERS

Another issue which involved a social change connected with gender caused the language some problems along the way, although the final effect was not at all dramatic. Before the 1960s it was not considered respectable for members of the opposite sex to live together unless they were married. Attitudes to unmarried sex changed from the 1960s, partly, it must be said, because of the introduction of the contraceptive pill. From then on, more and more members of the opposite sex took to living together without taking any marriage vows.

This involved a linguistic problem that people were much preoccupied with during the late 1970s and early 1980s. How do you introduce someone you are living with but who is not your husband or wife? Believe it or not, this was a question that many people, including several language experts, agonized over at the time.

Spouse was obviously just as inappropriate as husband or wife, while calling someone by the legal term, **cohabitee**, is enough to have them begging for marriage.

Boyfriend and **girlfriend** may have sounded a bit young in the particular circumstances and may even have suggested an unwanted degree of impermanence. **Lover** had the advantage of being able to be used to refer to both sexes, but it sounded rather racy and even illegal. We are talking here of respectable unmarried couples.

Partner was suggested quite early on, but it was rejected on the grounds that it properly belonged in a business relationship. Some strange alternatives were put forward. One of these was **significant other** which some people stuck with. However, this term mostly went on to mean a person who was influential or supportive in one's life (rather than someone who shared your house and bed as well as your life).

One of the strangest terms was **POSSLQ**, short for 'persons of the opposite sex sharing living quarters'. It seems extraordinary that this was given serious consideration by quite sensible people. Fortunately it did not last.

Someone uncovered the Scots word **bidie-in**, a word meaning 'a live-in partner' that was hitherto more or less restricted to the north-east of Scotland. For a time it enjoyed quite a lot of general attention in the British media, but this soon faded. It probably sounded far too homely and unsophisticated to be a real contender and it soon retreated back to its native heath. **Live-in** did not last very long either.

I mention these words that did not catch on simply to show you what a narrow escape language sometimes has. In this case it all came right in the end and we were left with **partner**, the word that is now still most commonly used. Its close association with business seemed not to matter after all. A lot of angst and argument could have been prevented if people had just settled on this term in the first place!

Vocabulary was not the only thing to change as the English language did its best to dispose of sexism – grammar, too, was affected (*see* **Desexing grammar** in Chapter 1). There can be no doubt that the movement to stamp out sexism in language achieved a great deal of success.

POLITICAL CORRECTNESS

To some extent, the movement to stamp out sexism got tangled up with the movement to impose **political correctness** (**PC**) on language, although the PC movement never did become the universal success that some people predicted.

Perhaps this lack of success was not all that surprising. For a start, the movement faced a major basic problem. Many people did not know what it was all about and many still do not know. Its very name was and is a barrier to understanding it. The term **political correctness** sounds as though it should mean something like 'in accordance with current or acceptable political beliefs or policy' and in fact it had a meaning of this kind in the 18th century.

However, by the time modern political correctness came into play around the mid 1980s in America, later in Britain, the term had little to do with what ordinary people regard as the meaning of 'political'. Instead it referred to a movement aimed at minimizing causing offence to others, especially when this was based on race, gender, religion, disability, age, occupation, etc.

This movement was not only aimed at language, but also at policy, behaviour and so on.

As you will see, it sounds as though this movement was based on very good intentions. It was an excellent idea to try to protect people from discrimination and insult. Sadly, this idea was taken to such ridiculous extremes that the term **political correctness** came to be regarded as a pejorative term, rather than a force for good.

It became something to poke fun at, rather than something to applaud and admire. If you mention the term **political correctness**, a great many people will come up with some humorous inventions based on the notion of political correctness.

Many of these involve the addition of the word **challenged**, as in:

chronologically challenged = old
morally challenged = criminal
follicularly challenged = bald.

The more extreme and unusual these inventions are, the funnier they seem – or so the user of the word thinks.

Of course political correctness had a serious purpose when it was introduced. It was intended to put a positive light on some kind of personal problem so that it did not seem to be as much of a disadvantage as might first appear. In its non-humorous sense it can be applied to someone who is disabled in the form **physically challenged**. Also, **visually challenged** is sometimes used to refer to people who are **partially sighted** or **visually impaired**.

There were several other PC suggestions put forward to describe people who are disabled, but they simply point to another problem that political correctness encountered. This was the fact that the very people that the movement was trying to protect did not much like the words that were suggested. Perhaps they found them patronizing. Perhaps they preferred to face their problems head on rather than pussyfoot around them. Whatever the reason, some expressions that were meant to put a positive light on a disability, such as **differently abled, otherly abled, otherwise abled** and **uniquely abled**, never really caught on.

REMOVING OFFENSIVE TERMS

The aim of political correctness was to avoid words and phrases that might be regarded as offensive to a particular section of society and it is a pity that it all went horribly wrong. However, the process of trying to avoid offensive words and phrases had been started long before the launch of the PC movement and it has had some success, particularly when related to race and nationality. Most dictionaries now, if they include such words at all, clearly indicate that they are considered to be offensive.

Some alterations to the language in this area involve a change of the name traditionally given to a particular group of people. For example, the indigenous people of the Arctic are now mostly known by the name **Inuit**, rather than by the name **Eskimo**, meaning 'eater of raw flesh'. The term **Inuit** is preferred by many of the people themselves, although the word **Eskimo** is still used.

There has also been a change of name for the people whose ancestors inhabited America before the arrival of Europeans. It seems unbelievable now, but, until fairly recently, these people were offensively and quite commonly known as **Red Indians**. This then became either **Indians** or **American Indians** and now the preferred term is **Native Americans** or **Native North Americans**.

THE COLOUR OF YOUR SKIN

The colour of a person's skin has caused many problems in language. Opinions as to what is an acceptable term for a dark-skinned person have differed, have changed and have changed back again. If you have lived through these changes this makes it difficult to decide what will be considered acceptable and what might give offence.

In the 1960s the word **coloured**, which grouped together everyone who was not white-skinned, was decreed to be offensive in Britain, but nowadays the term **Coloured** is used officially in South Africa to describe South Africans of mixed ethnic parentage or descent.

Political correctness was more successful in North America than it was in Britain. So it is that the terms **people of color** (**POCs**) and **women of color** (**WOCs**) are commonly used in America by ordinary people as well as bureaucrats.

Also in the 1960s, the term **black**, often spelt **Black**, became universally acceptable and was to be found in such expressions as *black power*. It was also used as a noun to refer to a person. However, many Americans of African descent prefer the term **African American**.

AGEISM

There have been many changes in society as the decades have gone by. One of these changes involves the length of the average allotted lifespan. Because of major advances in medical diagnosis and treatment, a great many people are living longer than previous generations did. Many of them remain fit and lively until they are quite old, but they do not feel old and they do not like to be called **old**. Baby boomers, the many people born in the years just after the Second World War, have been used to getting their own way, largely because there are so many of them. If they did not want to be called **old** then they would be called something more appropriate, but what?

Elderly is not much better than **old**, although it is considered to be more polite. Both words suggest that the person so described is a bit dated and might consider sitting by the fire knitting or reading a newspaper rather than going on a cruise. Perhaps **older** (attached to **people**) is the best option here. After all, practically everyone is older than someone else. Who can possibly object to the phrase **older people**? Almost certainly a good many can and will, but we shall move swiftly on.

It is as well not to talk of **the old**. This lumps people together and suggests that individually they do not matter. The same is true of expressions such as **the poor**, **the deaf** and **the blind**. *See* **Which word?** in Chapter 8.

For a while **OAP** was thought to be a suitable term for an older person. It might even have been regarded as an affectionate term, if you ignored the fact that it is an abbreviation for **old age pensioner**. **Old age pensioner** does not sound at all affectionate. Some language commentators have said that the expression is often used to suggest dependency on others, the feeling being that old age pensioners have somehow to be helped along by the rest of us. The baby boomers would not like that at all, even although many old age pensioners are reliant on the state benefit known as the **old age pension**.

I am always puzzled when media presenters, as they are wont to do, talk of **pensioners** and then reveal that they are talking of people over 55 or 60, or sometimes even over 50. They have to be talking about people who are in the enviable position of having a private pension which they can take at these ages. Successive governments seem to try and increase the age at which the state pension is paid. Who knows where that will end?

The Americans never did take to the term **OAP**, or, for that matter, its longer form **old age pensioner**. Instead, they opted for **senior citizen**. Unfortunately, I cannot help thinking of that in terms of the classroom and the playground, especially now that **senior** has gradually taken over from **senior citizen** in the States. Meanwhile, British English seems to be embracing **senior citizen**.

I have a particular dislike of ultra-jolly people, compères at concerts and the like, who describe **older people** as **80** or **90** (or so) **years young**. I am not too keen on the phrase **children of all ages** either.

In some cases, efforts to remove discrimination from language have been successful. However, in some ways by changing the language we are simply paying lip service to the removal of discrimination which unfortunately still flourishes in society to this day.

7

VEXING VERBS

The verb is usually the most important part of a sentence and so it is essential that you get it right. Now, there is nothing quite so off-putting as someone telling you right at the start of something that it can be very difficult. However, I feel that I have to do this on the subject of verbs. There is no point in lying to you. Verbs are hard work. They fulfil a number of functions in sentences, such as tense and mood, and all of these functions can give rise to problems. You have been warned!

Some of you may have put a lot of hard work into verbs already but have forgotten some of what you have learnt, or you may have not quite grasped the information first time around. For you the comments that follow will act as a kind of refresher course or give you some more guidance through the jungle that is verbs.

Hopefully, those of you who are still on the nursery slopes of verbs will also find them useful as a starting point.

WHAT IS A VERB?

In primary school some children are told that a verb is a 'doing word'. To some extent this is true but it is not the full story. Verbs are 'doing words' in the sense that they express action. In the following sentences the words **walk** and **listen** are both verbs:

They always walk to school.

Please listen carefully.

However, verbs can also be said to be 'being' words, in that they indicate a condition or a state. In this situation they do not actually refer to an action, but simply act as a connection between the subject and the other parts of the sentence that relate to it. In the following sentences the words **is** and **seems** are both verbs:

She is a very beautiful woman.

He seems an honest man.

I have indicated above that the functions of verbs can cause problems, but you do not get as far as that before you come across problems. The very forms of verbs can themselves cause headaches. The verbs that cause fewest problems in this respect are known as **regular verbs** because they follow a set, regular pattern – except when there are exceptions!

In order to understand what this pattern involves, you need to know something about **tenses**. With reference to verbs, the word **tense** indicates the time at which an action takes place. If the action is taking place now the verb is in the **present tense**, as in:

They live next door to us.

We are making cakes.

If the action has taken place in the past the verb is in the **past tense**, as in:

The children played in the park yesterday.

He once loved her.

If the action referred to is likely to happen in the future the verb is in the **future tense**, as in:

She will be very pleased to see you.

You also need to know what a **participle** is or does. You probably know this already but you may need reminding. The **past participle** is used with parts of the verb **have** to form the **perfect tense**, also known as the **present perfect tense**, as in:

They have bought a new house.

She has taken her child to the doctor.

In the first sentence **bought** is the past participle of the verb **buy** and in the second sentence **taken** is the past participle of the verb **take**.

The past participle is also used to form the **pluperfect tense,** also known as the **past perfect tense,** as in:

We had brought a packed lunch with us.

He had hidden the jewels in a cave.

In the first sentence **brought** is the past participle of the verb **bring** and in the second sentence **hidden** is the past participle of the verb **hide.**

The **present participle** is formed by adding **–ing** to the **infinitive** or **base form,** as in walking. The present participle is used with parts of the verb **be** to form the **present continuous tense,** as in:

We are walking to work.

You are snoring.

The **infinitive** or **base form** of a verb gives no indication of person, number or tense. The infinitive is often preceded by the word **to,** as in:

She wanted to sing.

They refused to go.

REGULAR VERBS

In regular verbs the ending **–ed** is added to the infinitive or base form of the verb in order to form the past tense and the past participle. Therefore **worked** is the past tense of the verb **work.**

If the verb already ends in **e** then only **–d** is added. Therefore **loved** is the past tense of the verb **love.**

When the infinitive or base form ends in **–ch, –ss** *or* **–x,** **–ed** is added, as in *march/marched* and *toss/tossed.*

When the infinitive or base form ends in **–y,** the **y** changes to **i** before **–ed** is added, as in *try/tried* and *marry/married.*

The present participle of regular verbs is formed by adding **–ing** to the infinitive or base form, as in *laugh/laughing* and *walk/ walking.*

If the base form ends in **–e**, the **e** is mostly dropped when the **–ing** is added, as in *dare/daring* and *change/changing*.

Another feature of regular verbs is that the third person singular of their present tense is formed by adding **–s** to the infinitive or base form, as in:

He plays football.

It seems obvious.

So far so good. All this seems fairly straightforward, but I have not yet mentioned **spelling** with reference to regular verbs and this can cause a few problems. Here are some rules that you need to know about.

SPELLING RULES FOR REGULAR VERBS

1   To form the present tense when the infinitive or base form ends in **–ch**, **–ss** *or* **–x**, **–es** is added rather than just **–s** , as in *march/marches* and *toss/tosses*. When the base form ends in **–y**, the **y** changes to **i** before the **–es** is added, as in *try/tries* and *cry/cries*.

2   To form the present participle when the infinitive or base form ends in **–e**, the **e** is removed from the infinitive or base form before adding **–ing**, as *manage/managing* and *rummage/rummaging*. Note that **ageing** can also be correctly spelt **aging**.

3   When a verb consists of one syllable and ends in a single consonant which is preceded by a single vowel, you double the consonant when adding **–ed** to form the past tense or past participle, or **–ing** to form the present participle, as with *drop/dropped/dropping* and *pat/patted/patting*. This sounds complicated but I assure you that it does make sense if you read it enough times.

4   When a verb consists of more than one syllable and ends in a single consonant preceded by a single vowel, you double the consonant if the word is pronounced with the stress is on the last syllable to form the past tense or past participle and the present participle. Examples include *refer/referred/referring*

and *transmit/transmitted/transmitting*. I promise you that this really does make sense. Start again and read slowly.

Just to make life more difficult there are some exceptions to this rule. One of them concerns the letter **l**. For this see rule 5 below. Other exceptions include *worshipped/worshipping* and *handicapped* where you double the **p** even though the stress is on the first syllable.

5 When the verb ends in **–l** then you double the letter **l** when forming the past participle or past tense or when you add **–ing** to form the present participle, even when the stress is *not* on the final syllable, as in *travel/travelled/travelling* and *level/levelled/levelling*. To make matters more complicated, American English does not follow this rule. It has *traveled/traveling* where British English has *travelled/travelling*. Watch out for this if you read a lot of American novels.

Note that some of these spelling rules do not apply only to regular verbs but they cause particular problems with reference to them.

COMMON ERRORS INVOLVING REGULAR VERBS

These often involve spelling errors.

- Forgetting to remove the **–e** from infinitive or base forms before adding **–ing** when forming the present participle. For example writing **judgeing** instead of **judging**. *See* Rule 2 on page 157.

- Forgetting to double the final consonant when forming the past tense or present participle of verbs such as **rot** or **pet**. Do not write **roted** or **peting**. These are wrong. **Rotted** and **petting** are the correct forms. *See* Rule 3 on page 157.

- Forgetting to double the final consonant in the past tenses or present participles of such words as **prefer** and **commit**. Do not write **prefered/prefering** or **commited/commiting**. These are wrong. **Preferred/preferring** and **committed/committing** are the correct forms. *See* Rule 4 on page 157.

- Forgetting to double the **–r** in the past tense and present participle of the verb **occur**. These should be spelt **occurred** and **occurring**. A word of warning. While you are trying to remember to double the letter **r**, you need to remember that the letter **c** should also be doubled.

- Doubling the **–r** in the past tense of the verb **offer**. **Offerred** is wrong because the stress on **offer** is not on the last syllable. **Offered** is correct. *See* Rule 4 on page 157.

- Doubling the **–p** in the present participle of the verb **develop**, *as in* **developping**, because the stress is not on the last syllable. **Developing** is correct. *See* Rule 4 on page 157.

- Forgetting to double the **–l** when forming the past participle or present participle of verbs such as **travel** and **level**. Do not write **marveled** or **appaling**. These are wrong. **Marvelled** and **appalling** are the correct forms. *See* Rule 5 on page 158.

- Forgetting to double the **–p** in **worshipped/worshipping**. This is an exception to Rule 4 on page 157. The form with the single letter **p** is correct use in American English (**worshiped/worshiping**).

- Doubling the **–t** in the past participle, past tense and present participle of the verb **benefit** as in **benefitted/benefitting**. These are wrong because the stress is not on the *first* syllable of the word **benefit**. They should be spelt **benefited** and **benefiting**.

There are plenty of examples of correct usage in italics in the two passages that follow.

GETTING AROUND

When we were there we *travelled* everywhere by train and could not help *marvelling* at how efficient their rail system is. We thought of taking our car over there, but we have both *committed* ourselves to helping to save the environment. Mind you, we were quite *appalled* at the cost of the train tickets. It *occurred* to me too late that the friend we were visiting had *referred* to this in one of her letters. Indeed, she had *offered* to buy our tickets locally for us, but I had refused. I thought it would not have *mattered*, but we found out that purchasing tickets locally in advance is much cheaper. Our travel budget would have *benefited* greatly from saving money like that.

RETURNING HOME

As I turned the key in the door, I was aware of such a terrible smell that I *dropped* the key. I rushed to the kitchen and found that all the vegetables in the fridge had *rotted*. The door had not been shut properly. It must have been open since we left to go on holiday two weeks ago. My son was supposed to make regular trips to the house but something must have *cropped* up. My wife, who was *patting the dog,* was *developing* a cold and she was lucky enough not be able to smell very well. I hastily gathered up the food from the fridge and *tossed* it into the bin at the back of the house. I then noticed a great pile of newspapers behind the front door. Our son had not *cancelled* them. I needed a cup of coffee desperately – or maybe something stronger!

IRREGULAR VERBS

If you think that regular verbs are difficult, you should prepare yourself for something much worse! As you might expect from their name, irregular verbs do not follow the pattern of regular verbs. They fall into several different categories, the rules of which are listed below. The information given is designed to simply jog your memory and help you reinforce what you already know but may have forgotten.

RULES FOR IRREGULAR VERBS

1   In some irregular verbs the past tense and the past participle both take the same form as the infinitive or base form, as in *cut/cut*, *bet/bet*, *hit/hit* and *put/put*.

2   Some irregular verbs have two past tenses and two past participles, both sets having the same form, as in *burned/burnt*, *dreamed/dreamt* and *spoiled/spoilt*.

3   Some irregular verbs have past tenses and past participles which have the same form as each other and do not end in **–ed**, as in *hold/held/held*, *keep/kept/kept* and *teach/taught/taught*.

4   Some irregular verbs have a past tense which, in common with those of regular verbs, ends in **–ed** or **–d**, whichever is relevant. However in this category the verb has two possible past participles, one of which is the same as the past tense and the other of which takes a different form. For example, the verb **show** has the past tense **showed** and the two past participles **showed** and **shown**, and the verb **prove** has the past tense **proved** and the past participles **proved** and **proven**.

5   Some irregular verbs have a past tense and a past participle which are different from each other and different from the infinitive or base form. For example the verb **draw** has the past tense **drew** and the past participle **drawn**, the verb **grow** has the past tense **grew** and the past participle **grown**, and the verb **swim** has the past tense **swam** and the past participle **swum**.

If you have read through all this and felt completely overwhelmed, do not worry and do not feel inadequate. It is not you. It is them. Irregular verbs are acknowledged to be one of the most difficult aspects of English grammar. There is only one thing to do with them. You have to grit your teeth and learn them. It will be worth it in the end. You'll see. Lists of irregular verbs in their different forms can be found on page 178.

COMMON ERRORS INVOLVING IRREGULAR VERBS

- Many of the errors involve the verbs which have been assigned to category 5 above. Some errors involve using the past participle form of one of these verbs wrongly when it is the past tense that is the correct form in the context, as in I swum (past participle) *in the lake yesterday* instead of correctly writing *I swam* (past tense) *in the lake yesterday* and wrongly writing *the phone only rung* (past participle) *once* instead of correctly writing *the phone only rang* (past tense) *once*.

- Sometimes it is the other way round. Some errors involve using the past tense form wrongly when it is the past participle that is the correct form in the context, as in *the ship had sank off the coast of Ireland* instead of correctly writing *the ship had sunk off the coast of Ireland*.

- Using **beat**, the past tense of the verb **beat**, in contexts where the past participle **beaten** should be used, as in *we've beat* (past tense) *them three times this season* instead of correctly writing *we've beaten* (past participle) *them three times this season.*

- Using **bit**, the past tense of the verb **bite**, in contexts where the past participle **bitten** should be used. It is wrong to write *her dog has bit* (past tense) *the postman.* The correct form is *her dog has bitten* (past participle) *the postman.*

- Using **gotten** instead of **got** as the past participle of the verb **get** in British English. To write *they have gotten very friendly just recently* or *they had gotten what they deserved* is currently considered wrong, but it is growing in popularity because of the influence of American films and books. The influence of American English has been strengthened by the fact that many learners of English now learn American English rather than British English.

- Using **dove** instead of **dived** as the past tense of the verb **dive** in British English. In American English both **dove** and **dived** are acceptable. *The boy dove into the pool* is considered correct in American English but wrong in British English. *The boy dived into the pool* is correct in British English.

- One of the most common errors involves the verb **do**. People frequently misuse **done** (past participle), wrongly writing *he done wrong and should be punished*, when the correct form of this is either *he has done wrong and should be punished* or *he did wrong and should be punished.* This mistake is more common in spoken English.

The passages that follow provide examples of irregular verbs in use.

MORE OF A HINDRANCE THAN A HELP

Mr Jackson had *learned* that his friends' children all helped with the housework and he *thought* that his three children should do the same. Unfortunately, it was not working out very well. Jane was helping to cook dinner, but she had *spilled/spilt* a bottle of cooking oil on the kitchen floor and had then *burned/burnt* the sausages. Dinner had definitely been *spoiled/spoilt*. Meanwhile Jack had *mowed/mown* the lawn and discovered he had an allergy to freshly cut grass. The area around his eyes had *swelled up/swollen up* and he kept sneezing.

He *had broken* the lawnmower, but he said that it *broke* by itself. Sue *chose* to go shopping and now wished she *had chosen* some other task. She *forgot* several items and was nearly home when she realized it. Her mother would not be pleased that she *had forgotten* so many things. Still her mother *forgave* people easily. She *had* already *forgiven* Jack and Jane for their mistakes. Sue was right. Furthermore, her mother had decided that she would rather not have her children's help around the house. She *had* always *known* the whole thing would be a disaster. She *knew* her children too well!

A TRAGEDY AT SEA

The fishing boat got into difficulties in the storm when it was within sight of the island. When it *sank* quite suddenly many of the crew *swam* ashore. If the ship *had sunk* any further out to sea there would have been more fatalities. Possibly there would have been more survivors if more men *had swum* ashore right away instead of taking time to get the lifeboat out. At least that is what one of the crew *wrote* in a letter to his family. He *had* also *written* to the families of those who had drowned simply to send his condolences. Many of the survivors *gave* money towards the purchase of a large wreath and they *had given* this to the grieving families on the day of the funeral.

ANTIQUES FOR SALE

John did not sell the house which he inherited from his aunt, but he *sold* most of the things that were in it. He said that he *had sold* these for two reasons. They were too old-fashioned for his taste and he needed the money which he *got* for them. In fact, he *had got* quite a lot of money from the sale. When John's aunt was young she was a keen collector of antiques and *had spent* most of her money on these. As she got older, she *spent* less on them, but she still had a valuable collection. She *had put* very little money into keeping the house in good repair. Now John *put* the money from the sale of the antiques into doing just that.

A MISUNDERSTANDING

I couldn't believe it. My boyfriend Tom's breath *stank* of alcohol and he *had driven* home. Tom *drove* to and from work every day and before I *met* him he had frequently had a few drinks with his workmates before setting out for home. Before he moved in with me he *had sworn* that he would never drink and drive again. I *swore* that I would throw him out if he ever did.

My best friend was killed by a drink-driver two years ago. She always *rode* her bike to university and she *had* just *ridden* out of the campus onto the main road when a car struck her. She died a few hours later in hospital. The driver was so drunk that he *had struck* her without even noticing. It seemed impossible.

From then on I *had worn* a badge warning people of the dangers of drink-driving. Tom *wore* one too, but it obviously didn't mean very much to him. I was so angry that I *tore* the badge from his jacket. In fact I saw that I *had torn* a bit of the jacket as well.

So far my boyfriend *had* not *spoken* a word. He now *spoke* and I *realized* that I *had made* a huge mistake. I *had lost* my temper before checking the facts. Tom's teetotal friend Jack had driven Tom home in Tom's car. That is how I *lost* that particular boyfriend!

ASPECTS OF VERBS
LIKELY TO CAUSE PROBLEMS

PARTICIPLES AND PARTICIPIAL PHRASES

A **participial phrase** contains a **participle** of a verb, whether present participle or past participle. Participial phrases can be used to cement the parts of a sentence together, as in:

> *Strolling along the woodland path, the visitors admired the brightly coloured spring flowers.*

In the sentence above the participial phrase beginning with the present participle *Strolling* refers to the subject of the sentence, *the visitors*, and is placed right next to it.

COMMON ERRORS INVOLVING PARTICIPLES

Avoid the dangling participle

The best place to put a participial phrase is next to the noun to which it refers. A **dangling** or **hanging participle** refers to a participle that is not attached to any word in the sentence. It is just 'dangling' there, as in:

> *Lying on the beach, summer was nearly at an end.*

Lying is certainly a present participle and it begins the participial phrase *Lying on the beach*. The trouble is that this phrase should refer to a person, but it seems to be referring to *summer*. This does not make sense. The participle is dangling there without purpose. In order to get the sentence to make sense we have to reword it, as in:

> *Lying on the beach, the young sun-worshippers felt that summer was nearly at an end.*

Lying now refers to the subject of the sentence, *the young sun-worshippers*. It is no longer dangling.

Another example of a dangling participle occurs in the following sentence:

> *Travelling north, the landscape became more and*
> *more bleak.*

Travelling is a present participle and it begins the participial phrase *Travelling north*. But the participial phrase seems to be referring to the *landscape*, which does not make sense. The *landscape* has been there for thousands of years and is not travelling anywhere. The participial phrase has to be attached to a person or something that is capable of travelling. The participle is dangling there without purpose.

In order to get the sentence to make sense, we have to reword it, as in:

> *Travelling north, the explorers saw that the*
> *landscape was getting more and more bleak.*

Travelling now refers to the subject of the sentence, *the explorers*. It is no longer dangling.

Avoid the misrelated participle

Sometimes participles are either wrongly or ambiguously placed. These are often known as misrelated participles, although some people also call these dangling participles, as in:

> *In the distance we could see, driving through the*
> *mountain pass, a small group of soldiers.*

This sentence is potentially ambiguous. Are *we* driving through the mountains or is it *the small group of soldiers* that are doing the driving? It is important that you attach the participle to the appropriate noun to avoid confusion and remove any possibility of ambiguity, as in:

> *Driving through the mountain pass, we could see in*
> *the distance a small group of soldiers.*

–ING FORM OF VERBS

The part of a verb ending in **–ing** can either be a present participle or it can be a **verbal noun**, also known as a **gerund**. It depends on the context.

In the sentence

> *I am walking in the park.*

the word *walking* is a present participle, while in the sentence

> *Walking is an excellent form of exercise.*

walking is a verbal noun or gerund. In this sentence the verbal noun or gerund *walking* is the subject of the sentence, but a verbal noun or gerund can also be the object of a sentence, as in:

> *He has taken up walking in order to get fit.*

The word **gerund** is now an unfamiliar word to many native speakers and is generally regarded as being difficult. There is one aspect of verbal nouns or gerunds that causes particular problems. According to traditional grammar, nouns or pronouns which qualify verbal nouns or gerunds should be in the possessive case. This means that the sentence

> *My parents strongly object to **my** smoking in their house.*

is, according to traditional grammar, considered correct, whereas the sentence

> *My parents strongly object to **me** smoking in their house.*

is considered wrong. Likewise, the following sentence

> *Apparently, her husband does not like **your** going round there.*

is, according to traditional grammar, considered correct, whereas the sentence

> *Apparently, her husband does not like **you** going round there*

is considered incorrect.

The trouble is that many people have difficulty in understanding this, and it sounds more natural to them to use the second version of each of the above sentences. The result is that more and more people are opting for it although such usage is ungrammatical. It is one of those cases in modern English where what sounds natural is taking precedence over what is grammatically correct. However, this use is best confined to spoken English and informal written English.

COMMON ERRORS INVOLVING GERUNDS

Forgetting in formal contexts to use the possessive case in sentences such as:

*My parents hate **my** smoking in their house.*

It is grammatically correct to use the possessive case, although in spoken and less formal written contexts many people now use:

*My parents hate **me** smoking in their house.*

VERB AGREEMENT

Verb agreement is also known as **concord** and refers to the fact that a verb must 'agree' with the appropriate subject in number. The word **number** is used to indicate whether the form of a word refers to one thing or more than one thing. Number agreement indicates that a singular noun is usually accompanied by a singular verb, as in:

The bus to the city runs every two hours.

While a plural noun is usually accompanied by a plural verb, as in:

Buses to the city are not very reliable.

COMMON ERRORS INVOLVING NUMBER AGREEMENT

* Usually two singular nouns joined together with **and** take a plural verb, as in:

Tom and Jane are going to the party.

Remember, however, that when the subject is made up of two or more singular nouns connected by a phrase which, in some way, emphasizes the 'togetherness' of the nouns, such as *together with*, *as well as*, *with* and *plus,* the verb takes the singular form, as in:

The boy's father, together with his elder sister, is going to visit him in hospital.

- Formerly it was the case that, when the subject takes the form of a singular noun linked to a plural noun by **of**, as in *a number of issues*, this had to be accompanied by a singular verb, as in:

A number of serious issues has to be taken into consideration.

If you used a plural verb in this context it was considered wrong. This is no longer the case. Nowadays, many people use a plural verb in such a situation, as in:

A number of serious issues have to be taken into consideration.

In other words, they make the verb agree with the nearest noun, in this case *issues* rather than *number*. Since this sounds more natural it is becoming more and more common, although it is grammatically wrong. You could say that common sense is prevailing.

- Take care with **group** or **collective nouns**, such as *committee*, *family*, *government* and *jury*. They can cause problems in relation to verb agreement. Some of these can be accompanied by either a singular or plural verb depending on the context. It all depends on whether you wish to emphasize the unity of the relevant noun, or whether you wish to emphasize the individual components that go to make up the noun. In the first case you would opt for a singular verb, while in the second case you would opt for a plural verb.

For example, if you are thinking of the family as a unit you might say:

The family is the most important influence in a young child's life.

If you are considering the components of a family you might say:

> *His family are coming from various parts of the*
> *world to celebrate his eightieth birthday with him.*

This distinction can be very difficult to get your head round and it can lead to a great deal of puzzlement and confusion. It can sometimes be difficult to decide which meaning you have in mind. Most people go on instinct or on what they think sounds best. It is a much simpler issue in American English, where such group or collective nouns are treated as singular.

- Remember that **indefinite pronouns**, such as *anyone*, *someone*, *everyone* and *no one,* should be accompanied by a singular verb, as in:

> *Everyone is welcome to attend the opening party.*

> *Either of the flats is suitable.*

> *Neither of them has a job.*

- Remember that if there is a combination of singular and plural subjects in the **either … or** construction, the verb agrees with the noun nearest to it, as in:

> *Either my brother or my parents are giving me a lift*
> *to the airport.*

> *Either his friends or his cousin is to blame for the*
> *damage to his car.*

The same is true of the *neither … nor* construction, as in:

> *Neither my sisters nor my brother has been invited.*

MOOD

Mood is one of the categories into which verbs are divided. It gets its name from the fact that it was thought to show the attitude or viewpoint that a particular verb indicated.

The moods are the **indicative mood**, the **imperative mood** and the **subjunctive mood**, but the only one of these that causes any problems is the **subjunctive**.

As far as most verbs are concerned the subjunctive form of the verb is the same as its basic form except that the third person singular leaves off the –s ending, e.g. **depart** instead of **departs**.

However the verb **be** has the past tense subjunctive **were** and its present subjunctive is **be**.

The subjunctive is used in modern English to express hypothetical statements, often beginning with the conjunction *if*.

In the following sentences the verb **were** is in the subjunctive mood:

> *If I were him I would look for another job.*

> *If I were Jack's mother I would be very disappointed in him.*

The subjunctive is also used in certain clauses, often beginning with **that**, which express a wish, demand or recommendation, as in:

> *I insist that she leave immediately.*

> *We suggest that he look for another job.*

> *The judge recommends that he be imprisoned for life.*

Because many people nowadays are not familiar with the word **subjunctive**, and, even if they are, do not understand what it is, its use is fading, except in very formal contexts. This is partly because people find that sentences using the subjunctive sound rather stilted and unnatural. It often takes a long time, but in the end, the will of the people sometimes dictates what happens to language.

If you are writing something formal and do not wish to use the subjunctive you can always use the verb **should** instead, as in the sentence

> *The judge recommends that he should be imprisoned for life.*

rather than

> *The judge recommends that he be imprisoned for life.*

VOICE

Voice, with reference to verbs, has nothing to do with the vocal cords. Instead, it refers to two ways of looking at the action of verbs. Verbs which take an object, called **transitive verbs**, can either be in the **active voice** or the **passive voice**.

In the case of the active voice the subject performs the action described by the verb in a sentence, as in:

The boy threw the ball.

In the case of the passive voice the subject in a sentence is the recipient of the action described by the verb, i.e. the object of the verb in an active sentence becomes the subject in a passive sentence, as in:

The ball was thrown by the boy.

COMMON ERRORS INVOLVING THE PASSIVE VOICE

* Be careful how you use the passive voice. In particular, do not overuse it. The active voice suits its name. Verbs in the active voice move the action of a piece of writing on, so to speak. They are more direct and more forceful and they are often clearer and shorter. Sentences with verbs in the passive voice are often less direct and, by their very nature, can be longer and less clear. Sometimes they can slow the action down, and research shows that readers take longer to understand sentences with verbs in the passive voice than sentences with verbs in the active voice. A sentence with a verb in the active voice actually identifies the person who was responsible for the action so there is little possibility of vagueness or ambiguity, as in:

Jack broke the window.

A sentence with a verb in the passive voice can describe an action without identifying the person who is responsible for it and this leaves room for vagueness or ambiguity, as in:

The window was broken.

- However, do not be afraid of the passive voice. Some people treat it as though it were some kind of monster that has to be avoided at all costs. This is not true. There is a time and a place for everything, including the passive voice. For example, you might want to report some kind of action which you know has been committed without knowing who committed it, as in:

  The woman was murdered early this morning.

  This sounds better than:

  Someone murdered the woman early this morning.

  Use the passive voice sparingly and avoid it as much as possible until you have reasonably well-honed writing skills. But remember that it can be a useful stylistic device.
- If you are writing something of an academic nature or if you are writing something that is meant to be informative, do not use phrases in the passive voice too often. The phrases in the passive voice that follow, for example, are frequently too vague to be appropriate in that kind of writing:

  It is now widely believed that ...

  It has been shown by research that ...

  Studies show that ...

TENSE

The **tense** of a verb indicates the time at which an action takes place.

COMMON ERRORS INVOLVING TENSE

- Many errors involving tense concern the parts of irregular verbs, especially the past participles and the past tenses. *See* **Common errors involving irregular verbs** on page 161.
- A common error is to use the verb **was** when you mean the verb **were,** as in:

  We was sure we would win.

This is wrong. It should be:

We were sure we would win.

This mistake is common in spoken English and in very informal written English.

- Try not to confuse the simple present tense and the continuous present tense, also known as the progressive present tense.

  The continuous present tense is used when you are referring to something that is happening at that very moment, or when you are referring to an action continuing over a period of time, including the present, and not complete at the time you are referring to it. The continuous present tense is more commonly used in everyday English than the present tense. Learners of English, in particular, can have problems with this tense.

  If, for example, someone is preparing a meal as you speak, you would say:

  He is cooking (continuous present tense) *tonight's meal in the kitchen.*

  not

  He cooks (simple present tense) *tonight's meal in the kitchen.*

  You would say:

  We are just reaching the outskirts of the city now.

  not

  We reach the outskirts of the city now.

- A similar confusion can arise between the simple past tense and the continuous past tense, also the progressive past tense.

- **will/shall.** Remember that the future tense is now commonly formed with **will** plus the infinitive form of the main verb, as in:

  I will see you there.

  They will drive up tomorrow.

Formerly, you had to choose between will and shall according to context. *See* **Which word?** in Chapter 8.

The word **shall** is sometimes used when questions are being asked or when suggestions are being made when these relate to the immediate situation, as in:

Shall I proceed?

In informal and relatively informal contexts the contracted form is used, as in:

What'll you have?

Remember that the simple present tense is sometimes used instead of the future tense, as in:

I leave for the States tomorrow.

MODAL VERBS

The main **modal verbs**, also called **modal auxiliary verbs**, are *can, could, may, might, will, shall, would, should, must* and *ought to*.

These verbs are used with main verbs to express a wide range of meanings including possibility, probability, ability, permission, prediction, requests, invitations, etc.

COMMON ERRORS INVOLVING MODAL VERBS

- **can/may**. In all but the most formal contexts **can** is now more normally used than **may**, as in:

  Can I come in?

  Can we go out to play?

  Using **can** in such situations is no longer regarded as an error. *See* **Which word?** in Chapter 8 page 197.

- **will/shall** *see* page 175.

- Do not write the word **of** instead of the verb **have** as part of a verb. There is a common tendency now for people to use *could of, should of, would of, must of,* etc, instead of the correct form *could have, should have, must have,* etc.

Doing so is grammatically quite wrong. Of course, except in formal contexts, it is all right to use the contracted forms of *could have, should have* and *would have, etc,* as in *could've, should've, would've, etc. See* **Which word?** in Chapter 8 page 197.

THE ANTI-VERB BRIGADE

There is something about some verbs that some people do not like in modern English usage. The creation of new verbs that end in **–ize** (or **–ise**) is a particular pet hate of many. This modern tendency began in the second part of the 20th century and one of the first of such verbs to record extreme levels of dislike was *privatize.* This means 'to transfer an industry, etc, from state ownership to private ownership' and there might have been a touch of political dissent there as well as linguistic disagreement.

A spate of verbs with the same ending followed with much protest. So we ended up with words such as *hospitalize, pedestrianize* and *institutionalize. Prioritize* was very unpopular when it first made an appearance but, as often happens, people got used to it, as we did to *decimalize* and *computerize.* The introduction of *incentivize* caused another storm of protest, but since its purpose is to motivate people by offering them high rewards, usually of a financial nature, those in the happy situation of being incentivized, such as bankers, are almost certainly not worried. More specialist **–ize** verbs, such as *weaponize,* have also reared their ugly heads. Let us hope the use of that particular verb does not become an everyday occurrence.

The habit of forming new verbs, now called 'verbing' or 'verbifying', by adding **–ize** was blamed on America, as many things are, but the **–ize** habit is in fact a very old one. It was a common practice of Thomas Nashe, the English dramatist, satirist and pamphleteer, and he was writing towards the end of the 16th century. He was apparently fond of such words as *superficialize* and *citizenize*!

Of course, not all new verbs are formed with the ending **–ize** (or **–ise**). Some of them simply use the form of the noun on which they are based. For example, in the following sentences the verb *tasked has come from the noun task, and the verb impacted* has come from the noun *impact*:

> *He was tasked with setting up a new marketing department.*

> *Online purchasing has impacted on many high-street shops.*

Both of these verbs send the blood pressure of some people soaring and yet neither of them is new. *Task* was first used as a verb in the 16th century and *impact* in the 17th century.

The age of the computer has brought many new verbs into the English language. They seem to have been well tolerated at first as long as they remained firmly in the technical field and did not spread into the general language. But inevitably some of these verbs have spread their wings to howls of protest from some. The verbs *input and access* met with particularly strong opposition when they first entered into the general language, but these and other new verbs, such as *bookmark, blog* and *Google, are now used by millions of people.*

Technological advances in general are occurring at a terrifying rate and advances in verbing are not far behind. Think of other new verbs like *text* from the world of mobile phones and the verbs friend and unfriend from Facebook.

They may have caused some controversy but for better or worse all of these verbs are now part of the English language's rich store of words.

SOME IRREGULAR VERBS

In the following list of irregular verbs the past tense and the past participle both take the same form as the infinitive or base form:

infinitive	past tense	past participle
bet	bet	bet
burst	burst	burst
cast	cast	cast

infinitive	past tense	past participle
cost	cost	cost
cut	cut	cut
hit	hit	hit
hurt	hurt	hurt
let	let	let
put	put	put
set	set	set
shed	shed	shed
shut	shut	shut
slit	slit	slit
split	split	split
spread	spread	spread

Some irregular verbs have two past tenses and two past participles which are the same. These include:

infinitive	past tense	past participle
burn	burned, burnt	burned, burnt
dream	dreamed, dreamt	dreamed, dreamt
dwell	dwelled, dwelt	dwelled, dwelt
hang	hanged, hung	hanged, hung
kneel	kneeled, knelt	kneeled, knelt
lean	leaned, leant	leaned, leant
leap	leaped, leapt	leaped, leapt
learn	learned, learnt	learned, learnt
light	lighted, lit	lighted, lit
smell	smelled, smelt	smelled, smelt
speed	speeded, sped	speeded, sped
spill	spilled, spilt	spilled, spilt
spoil	spoiled, spoilt	spoiled, spoilt
weave	weaved, woven	weaved, woven
wet	wetted, wet	wetted, wet

Some irregular verbs have past tenses that do not end in *–ed* and have the same form as the past participle. These include:

infinitive	past tense	past participle
bend	bent	bent
bleed	bled	bled
breed	bred	bred
build	built	built
cling	clung	clung
dig	dug	dug
feel	felt	felt
fight	fought	fought
find	found	found
flee	fled	fled
fling	flung	flung
get	got	got
grind	ground	ground
hear	heard	heard
hold	held	held
keep	kept	kept
lay	laid	laid
lead	led	led
leave	left	left
lend	lent	lent
lose	lost	lost
make	made	made
mean	meant	meant
meet	met	met
pay	paid	paid
rend	rent	rent
say	said	said
seek	sought	sought

infinitive	past tense	past participle
sell	sold	sold
send	sent	sent
shine	shone	shone
shoe	shod	shod
sit	sat	sat
sleep	slept	slept
slide	slid	slid
sling	slung	slung
slink	slunk	slunk
spend	spent	spent
stand	stood	stood
stick	stuck	stuck
sting	stung	stung
strike	struck	struck
string	strung	strung
sweep	swept	swept
swing	swung	swung
teach	taught	taught
tell	told	told
think	thought	thought
understand	understood	understood
weep	wept	wept
win	won	won
wring	wrung	wrung

Some irregular verbs have regular past tense forms but two possible past participles, one of which is regular. These include:

infinitive	past tense	past participle
mow	mowed	mowed, mown
prove	proved	proved, proven
sew	sewed	sewed, sewn
show	showed	showed, shown
sow	sowed	sowed, sown
swell	swelled	swelled, swollen

Some irregular verbs have past tenses and past participles that are different from each other and different from the infinitive. These include:

infinitive	past tense	past participle
arise	arose	arisen
awake	awoke	awoken
bear	bore	borne
begin	began	begun
bid	bade	bidden
bite	bit	bitten
blow	blew	blown
break	broke	broken
choose	chose	chosen
do	did	done
draw	drew	drawn
drink	drank	drunk
drive	drove	driven
eat	ate	eaten
fall	fell	fallen
fly	flew	flown
forbear	forbore	forborne
forbid	forbade	forbidden

infinitive	past tense	past participle
forgive	forgave	forgiven
forget	forgot	forgotten
forsake	forsook	forsaken
freeze	froze	frozen
forswear	forswore	forsworn
give	gave	given
go	went	gone
grow	grew	grown
hew	hewed	hewn
hide	hid	hidden
know	knew	known
lie	lay	lain
ride	rode	ridden
ring	rang	rung
saw	sawed	sawn
see	saw	seen
rise	rose	risen
shake	shook	shaken
shrink	shrank	shrunk
slay	slew	slain
speak	spoke	spoken
spring	sprang	sprung
steal	stole	stolen
stink	stank	stunk
strew	strewed	strewn
stride	strode	stridden
strive	strove	striven
swear	swore	sworn
swim	swam	swum
take	took	taken

tear	tore	torn
throw	threw	thrown
tread	trod	trodden
wake	woke	woken
wear	wore	worn
write	wrote	written

8

CONFUSION UPON CONFUSION

The English language has a huge vocabulary. This is obviously a good thing because it means that you have a wide choice of words at your fingertips to express what you want to say. However, it also means that is very easy to get confused when you are trying to select the right word for what you want to express.

There are various well-known pitfalls when it comes to making the right choice of word, but that does not make them any easier to avoid unless you have been made aware of them. My aim is to try to bring some of the potential stumbling blocks to your attention. Try and remember at least some of them, or at least remember to look them up when warning bells ring in your head. This will definitely save you problems in the future.

There are three categories of words which cause particular confusion. They are **homophones, homographs, homonyms**. They sound rather complicated and are exactly the kind of words that might make some of you switch off. If you do that please switch back on again! The words are easier to understand than you think. Anyway, you can forget the names of the categories as long as you remember the problems which they represent.

HOMOPHONES

The word **homophone** comes from the Greek word *homophonos*, which means having the same sound. This may have led more of you to switching off, but it gives a good indication of the nature of the problem with homophones. Homophones are pronounced in the same way as each other, but they have different meanings and spellings. They cause a good deal of confusion.

RP

A minor word of caution here regarding pronunciation. Strictly speaking, we are talking here of pronunciation according to RP. Learners of English will be well aware of this term. However, native speakers may have managed to ignore the existence of RP and gone on pronouncing words in their own sweet way.

Just for the record I should tell you, or remind you, that RP is short for Received Pronunciation. This name is given to the form of speech associated with educated people in the south of England and is used as a model of pronunciation in the teaching of English as a foreign language.

There are many accents in the UK and several forms of English other than British English, which do not conform to the rules of RP. Thus, words that are homophones as pronounced by RP speakers will not necessarily be homophones when they are pronounced by speakers of American English or by people speaking with, for example, a Scots accent.

Below are some examples of homophones. Sometimes only two words are involved, but sometimes there are three or four.

HOMOPHONE EXAMPLES

currant/current

The words **currant** and **current** have nothing in common except their pronunciation. **Currant** is a noun meaning 'a small dried grape used in baking', as in:

> *We need flour, butter, eggs and currants to make this cake.*

Current has a much wider range of meanings. As a noun it can be found in such contexts as *electric current, the current of a river* and *a current of cold air.* As an adjective it means 'belonging to the present time', as in *a current affairs programme on television* and *the current fashion in food.*

heal/heel

These words are pronounced in the same way but have very different meanings. Heal is a verb meaning 'to become or make healthy again', as in:

> *The wound has started to heal at last.*

Heel is the back part of a foot below the ankle, as in:

Her shoes were too tight and she got a blister on her heel.

hear/here

The words **hear** and **here** share a pronunciation but have different meanings. **Hear** is a verb meaning 'to become aware of sounds by means of your ears', as in:

She didn't hear the door bell because she is deaf.

Here is an adverb meaning 'this place', as in:

I'm not going anywhere. I'm staying right here.

rain/reign/rein

The words **rain, reign** and **rein** are pronounced alike but are otherwise unrelated. **Rain** is water that falls from the sky, as in:

We got very wet in the heavy rain.

Reign refers to the period of time when a king or queen is ruling, as in:

The Second World War took place during the reign of George VI.

Rein means 'a long narrow band of leather used to control a horse' and it is mostly found in the plural form, as in:

The rider let the reins fall from her hands as her horse came to a standstill.

right/rite/write/wright

These words are pronounced alike but are completely different in meaning.

As an adjective **right** has several meanings. It can mean 'correct', as in *the right answer* or *he turned out to be right*. It can also mean 'the opposite of left', as in:

He held it in his right hand.

As a noun **right** refers to something that you are legally, officially or morally allowed to do or have, as in:

You have no right to refuse us entry to this park.

The women's movement was established to protect the rights of women.

The word **rite** is a noun which refers to a ceremonial act that is always performed in the same way, often as part of a religious ceremony, as in *traditional funeral rites*.

The word **write** is a verb meaning 'to make letters, words or numbers on paper using a pen or pencil', as in *primary schoolchildren just learning to write*. It can also mean 'to set down words for others to read', as in:

I'm not going to phone them. I'm going to write them a letter.

The word **wright** is much less common than the other two words on this list. Usually it comes as the second part of a compound word which indicates someone who works at particular trade or job, as in *shipwright* and *playwright*.

HOMOGRAPHS

Homographs are words which have the same spelling but different meanings, and are pronounced differently.

HOMOGRAPH EXAMPLES

lead/lead

As you can see, these two words look exactly the same. They are spelt in the same way, but they are pronounced differently and they have totally different meanings. One of the words rhymes with *bead* and *feed* while the other rhymes with *red* and *fed*. The lead rhyming with *feed* is a verb whose primary meaning is 'to guide people somewhere by going in front of them', as in:

The mountain guide will lead the party of climbers safely to the summit.

The lead rhyming with *fed* is a noun which refers to a type of soft, heavy grey metal, as in:

> *Lead was once used to make water pipes but this*
> *practice was stopped as lead is poisonous.*

Note that the past participle of the verb lead is spelt *led* and it is pronounced like the metal.

row/row

Obviously these two words are spelt the same but they are pronounced differently and have totally different meanings.

One of the words rhymes with *low* and *mow* and is a noun meaning 'a number of people or things arranged in a line', as in:

> *There was a row of policemen blocking the entrance*
> *to the building.*

The other row rhymes with *cow* and *how* and is a noun meaning 'a quarrel or disagreement', as in:

> *The boy and his father were always having rows.*

minute/minute

Like the others words in this category, these words share a spelling but not a pronunciation and they have different meanings.

One of the words is pronounced *min-it*, with the stress on the first syllable. It is a noun referring to a unit of time, as in *60 minutes in an hour.*

The other word is an adjective. Its first part is pronounced to rhyme with *mine* and its second part is pronounced *yoot*, the stress being on the first syllable. This second word means 'extremely small', as in *minute amounts of poison.*

HOMONYMS

Homonyms are words which have the same spelling and the same pronunciation but they have different meanings. They are sometimes referred to as **multiple meaning words**. Below are some examples.

HOMONYM EXAMPLES

bill/bill

These two words are spelt and pronounced in the same way, but they have different meanings.

The first and more common bill refers to a piece of paper which shows how much money you owe someone for goods or services (although it also has other related meanings), as in:

> *I've just had a huge bill for repairs to the car.*

The second bill is quite unrelated to the first. It means 'a bird's beak', as in:

> *The thrush had a small worm hanging from its bill.*

calf/calf

These two nouns are spelt and pronounced in the same way, but they have different meanings.

One of the meanings of the word **calf** relates to animals. Commonly it refers to a young cow, although it can also refer to the young of some other animals, such as elephants.

The other meaning of **calf** relates to the human body and refers to the back part of the leg between the ankle and the back of the knee, as in:

> *She got cramp in her calf after dancing all night.*

swallow/swallow

These two words are spelt and pronounced in the same way, but they have different meanings.

One of these words is a noun used to refer to a kind of bird, as in:

> *It was the end of summer and swallows were*
> *getting ready to fly to warmer lands for the winter.*

The other swallow is a verb meaning 'to cause food or drink to go down your throat into your stomach', as in:

> *He had a very sore throat and could only swallow*
> *very small pieces of food.*

ORONYMS

It might be time to introduce a little light relief. A sequence of words, as in ice cream, that sounds the same as a different sequence of words, as in I scream, are sometimes used humorously or in word games and are called oronyms. The word **oronym** was apparently coined by Gyles Brandreth, wordsmith, broadcaster and former MP.

Oronyms include *ice cream* and *I scream*; *example* and *egg sample; four candles* and *fork handles; realize* and *real eyes*; and *depend* and *deep end.* Of course it sometimes depends on how you pronounce them.

What use are oronyms? Not a lot, really, but you might have fun making some up!

A MISCELLANY OF MISTAKES

There are a huge number of words that cause problems and they do not fall into any of the above categories. Sometimes confusion between words arises because they sound quite similar and they are both associated with the same theme. Some of the most problematic are discussed below.

SIMILAR BUT DISSIMILAR

continual/continuous
These two adjectives sound quite similar but have quite different meanings.

Continual means 'frequently repeated', as in:

> *Continual complaints from other residents were ignored by the students.*

Continuous means 'without a break', as in:

> *How do the factory workers put up with the continuous noise made by the machinery?*

adopted/adoptive
Another two adjectives in the same category are **adopted** and

adoptive. They also sound quite similar and they are both associated with the same theme, namely raising a child who is not your biological son or daughter.

Adopted is used to describe children who have been brought up by people other than their biological parents, as in:

> *The couple have two sons, one biological, one adopted.*

Adoptive is used to refer to adults who have done the adopting, as in:

> *She would love to try and get in contact with her biological mother, but she does not want to upset her much-loved adoptive mother.*

arbiter/arbitrator

Another two words which fall into a similar category are **arbiter** and **arbitrator**. The first part of the second word sounds like the first word and they both refer to a similar theme, that of judging.

The noun **arbiter** refers to someone or something with the power or influence to make decisions or judgements, as in:

> *The dress designer is very young but she is quickly becoming recognized as one of the leading arbiters of fashion.*

The noun **arbitrator** refers to someone appointed to settle differences in a dispute, as in:

> *Management and union leaders have failed to settle their differences and have called in an arbitrator to try to avoid a strike.*

Note that **arbiter** is one of those words that is in the process of changing. In modern usage it is occasionally used with the same meaning as **arbitrator**. This can only add to the confusion.

abuse/misuse

The words **abuse** and **misuse** also fall into the same category as the words dealt with above. In the case of **abuse** and **misuse** they share their second syllable and they both refer to the theme of use or treatment. Both are nouns that refer to a wrong use or treatment, but they are used in different contexts. Like **misuse**, the word **abuse** refers to improper or wrong use or treatment. The word **abuse**, however, is more likely to refer to something that is morally wrong, dangerous to health or illegal, as in *alcohol abuse; drug abuse; solvent abuse; the abuse of political power; physical abuse* and *sexual abuse*. The verb **abuse** has similar associations to that of the noun **abuse**, as in:

> *The politician was being investigated for abusing his power.*

Misuse usually refers to incorrect or inappropriate use, as in *misuse of the gym equipment* and *misuse of the communal garden.*

compulsory/compulsive
Another two words which fall into the category described above are **compulsory** and **compulsive**. Only the endings of these two adjectives are different and they both refer to something that must be done.

If something is **compulsory** there is a law or rule which says that it must be done or carried out, as in:

> *In that country it is compulsory to always carry identification documents.*

Compulsive refers to behaviour or a habit that is very difficult or impossible to stop or control, as in:

> *He is a compulsive gambler who has lost a fortune on betting on horses.*

industrial/industrious
The words **industrial** and **industrious** are both adjectives. They look and sound like each other, apart from their endings, and are liable to be confused. They both refer to work, but not the same meaning of work.

As you might expect, **industrial** has to do with industry in the sense of the business of making or producing goods, usually on a large scale, as in:

> *The land on which the houses were built was*
> *formerly an industrial site.*

Industrious is an adjective based on a much less common and more formal meaning of industry meaning 'hard work' or 'diligence', as in:

> *He was not as intelligent as some of the other*
> *students but he was very industrious and usually*
> *managed to do well in exams.*

immoral/immortal

Some words which get confused because they resemble each other quite closely and because they have a reasonably similar pronunciation do not belong to the same theme. They are actually unrelated.

Two such words are **immoral** and **immortal**. These two adjectives would be the same word but for the letter *t*, and this gives rise to confusion. What a difference one letter can make!

Immoral means 'morally wrong'. In other words, wrong according to the principles of what is considered to be right and wrong behaviour, as in:

> *It is immoral to make young children work long hours for*
> *very little pay in order to be able to export cheap goods.*

Immortal literally means 'living or existing forever', as in:

> *No one is immortal, although some people behave*
> *as though they think they are.*

Immortal can also be used to refer to something, such as a line of prose, poetry or song, that has become very famous and has lasted a very long time, as in:

> *Just think of the immortal line 'Tomorrow is*
> *another day'.*

persecute/prosecute

Two other words which are frequently confused are the verbs **persecute** and **prosecute**. Obviously, the confusion arises because the second part of each of them is the same. However, the problem lies in **per** and **pro**, their short first syllables.

As we have seen, these words have something in common in that they look quite like each other and, in fact, there is a degree of similarity in their pronunciation. There is also a degree of similarity in their theme but they are at opposite ends of the scale. The theme is fairness or justice. **Persecute** comes under the heading of 'unfairness' or 'lack of justice' in that it means 'to treat someone very unfairly and unjustly, and usually with great cruelty, over a long period of time'. This treatment often takes place on the grounds of political or religious beliefs, as in:

> *Many people were persecuted for their opposition to*
> *racial discrimination.*

Prosecute, on the other hand, is mostly on the side of fairness and justice, or at least we hope so. It means 'to charge someone with committing a crime and to try to show that they are guilty of it', as in:

> *There was a sign on the shop door saying*
> *'Shoplifters will be prosecuted'.*

chronic/acute

As you have seen, confusion with regard to words is often a result of the words, or parts of words, having a similar sound. Sometimes, however, the words do not sound or look like each other at all. They are completely different but they may very well relate to the same theme. The confusion created by the adjectives **chronic** and **acute** is a good example of this. Both **chronic** and **acute** frequently refer to a disease or illness. **Chronic** refers to a disease or illness that lasts a long time, frequently a period of several years, and often develops slowly, as in:

> *Many elderly people suffer from chronic arthritis*
> *and need long-term drug treatment.*

By contrast, **acute** refers to a disease that lasts a relatively short time and starts up quite suddenly, as in:

> *She has acute earache and needs some strong*
> *painkillers immediately.*

hire/rent

Hire and **rent** are another two words that get confused, although they do not resemble each other at all in appearance or sound. However, they both relate to the temporary use of something in exchange for payment. Sometimes whether you use **hire** or **rent** depends on how long the temporary use is likely to last.

Hire is more likely to be associated with short-term use, as in:

> *She thinks she might hire a wedding dress rather than buy one.*

Rent suggests a more long-term use, as in:

> *Their plan is to rent a flat for the two years that their college courses last.*

However, there is a problem. In American English **rent** is used in connection with short-term use as well as longer-term use. The American use is having some influence on British English, so that you will now find both *hire a car for the weekend* and *rent a car for the weekend* being commonly used. Isn't that typical? You just get something sorted out when it changes!

Note that the verb **charter**, rather than **hire** or **rent**, is used in connection with boats or planes, as in *charter a yacht*.

VARIABLE VERBS

Much confusion is caused by irregular verbs. This problem is dealt with in quite a lot of detail in Chapter 7, so have a look there for further information. Apart from anything else, you will find a helpful list of irregular verbs there. The irregular verbs that cause most problems, as far as this chapter is concerned, are those which fall under rule 5 in Chapter 7, page 161.

This section refers to those irregular verbs which have a past tense and a past participle which are different from each other and different from the infinitive or base form. For example the verb **draw** has the past tense **drew** and the past participle **drawn**, the verb **grow** has the past tense **grew** and the past participle **grown** and the verb **swim** has the past tense **swam** and the past participle **swum**.

hanged/hung

One of the most common pair of confused words relating to irregular verbs is **hanged** and **hung**. The verb **hang** has two possible past tenses and past participles, **hanged** and **hung**. Of these the form **hung** is by far the more common, as in:

We hung some decorations on the Christmas tree.

The form **hanged** is mostly used when related to execution by hanging someone from a rope or to suicide by the same means, as in:

The murderer was hanged.

This error has become so common that the distinction between the two words is in real danger of being forgotten.

got/gotten

A pair of words relating to irregular verbs has only relatively recently started causing confusion. The words are **got** and **gotten** and they are both past participles of the verb **get**.

Gotten used to be restricted to American English usage but I have noticed an increasing number of writers who are using the American version. Admittedly some of them have been writers who are publishing their own material as ebooks rather than having it carefully edited by trained publishers' editors, but it is certainly a sign of the times. See also page 162.

PERSONAL AND FAMILIAL CONFUSION

Sometimes problem words are a purely personal thing. Some people seem to see similarity, and so confusion, between words when no one else can spot this. One person I knew used to use the word **dislevelled** when she meant **dishevelled**, an adjective used of the hair or clothes to describe a state of untidiness. Although she was very well educated, she seemed totally unable to take on board that **dislevelled** was not the right word, or even a word at all!

Then I discovered that her mother, sister and grandmother all used the word **dislevelled** instead of **dishevelled**. It certainly seems to be the case that some word confusion is hereditary. A member of one generation gets hold of the wrong word and this is then passed down the line to succeeding generations. People learn the wrong word at their mother's knee and it sticks.

Dishevelled is not a word that you use every day, even if you come from a particularly untidy family, so it took me quite a long time to find this out. The family was generally low on males so I do not know if this linguistic habit was restricted to the female line.

I had another friend who persisted in using the word **munificent** when he meant **magnificent**. At least **munificent** is an actual word but its meaning is quite far from that of **magnificent**.

Munificent is an adjective meaning 'extremely generous' and **magnificent** is an adjective meaning 'impressive' or 'splendid'. Again, my friend was a very well-educated person and, indeed, a professional writer to trade. Whether or not his linguistic error was purely personal or whether it, too, came down through the generations I have no means of knowing as I never met any of his family.

PERENNIAL POSERS

Confusing words can be a purely personal or familial habit. But as far as the vast majority of words are concerned, the confusion is not restricted to one person or even to a few people. As far as these words are concerned, confusion is widespread and the confusion continues decade after decade. Some of these words have been discussed in what has gone before in this chapter, but that leaves a tremendous number of words that have not been covered.

WHICH WORD?

Below is a list in alphabetical order of words that commonly get confused. It is by no means comprehensive, but it will at least set you off in the right direction.

a/an

The indefinite article has the forms **a** and **an**. Although these words are very small they can cause a great deal of confusion. The form **a** is used before words or abbreviations that are pronounced with an initial consonant sound, as in *a box; a garden; a UFO;* and *a wall.*

The form **an** is used before words that begin with an initial vowel sound, as in *an apple; an igloo; an IOU* and *an ostrich.* Remember that it is the sound of the initial letter and not the spelling that determines whether the indefinite article should be **a** or **an**.

The form **a** is used before words beginning with the letter **u** when these are pronounced as though they began with the consonant **y**, as in *a unit* and *a union.*

The form **an** is used before words beginning with the letter **h** where this is not pronounced, as in *an heir* and *an hour.* Formerly the form **an** was commonly used before words beginning with the **h** sound which began with an unstressed syllable, as in *an historic victory* and *an hotel*, but in modern usage the form **a** is used in such cases, as in *a historic victory* and *a hotel.*

abuse/misuse
See page 191 under **A miscellany of mistakes.**

accessory/accessary
Although not spelt exactly alike, these words sound alike.

The noun **accessory** has two quite distinct meanings. The more common meaning is 'something additional to the main part' or 'an extra attachment'. It is often used in connection with fashion, meaning handbag, shoes, belt, scarf, etc, as in:

> *She wore a red dress with black accessories.*

The other meaning of **accessory** is used to refer to someone who helps someone else to do something, often something criminal, as in:

> *Police say that the bank robber must have had at least one accessory.*

What about the noun accessary? Well it was formerly the word used to refer to a partner in crime, but now **accessory** is the more common form. In this British English is following the practice of

American English. You might still come across **accessary** in some formal legal contexts.

adopted/adoptive

See page 190 under **A miscellany of mistakes.**

adverse/averse

These words look and sound quite alike but they are used in quite different ways. The adjective **adverse** usually goes before the abstract noun to which it refers, and means 'unfavourable' or 'hostile', as in:

> *The last thing we want is adverse publicity for our forthcoming exhibition.*

Averse is never placed before the noun to which it refers and is followed by the preposition **to**. **Averse to** means having a strong dislike for, as in:

> *They are not averse to the idea but they need more information before they make up their minds.*

advice/advise

These words look and sound quite alike and they both relate to telling someone what to do. However, **advice** is a noun, as in:

> *You should seek medical advice right away.*

While **advise** is a verb, as in:

> *I would advise you to make an appointment with a doctor right away.*

adviser/advisor

Both of these spellings for a word meaning 'someone who gives advice' are in common use in British English. In American English, **advisor** is the commoner form. Note that the adjective is always spelt **advisory**.

affect/effect

These words sound alike, especially when they are spoken quickly or carelessly, and they are frequently confused. In meaning they can both refer to influence or change, but **affect** is a verb and

effect is a noun.

The verb **affect** is used in such contexts as:

> *How did the war affect the economy?*

While the noun **effect** is used in such contexts as:

> *What was the effect of the war on the economy?*

The word **effect** can also be used as a verb in formal contexts meaning 'to bring about' or 'carry out', as in:

> *The army effected a quick retreat.*

afterwards/afterward

Many learners of English learn American English rather than British English and it is easy to get confused between the two. In British English **afterwards** is the usual form of the adverb meaning 'later' or 'after something else has happened', as in:

> *He thought that he had done well in the interview and he was told afterwards that he very nearly got the job.*

In American English this adverb often takes the form **afterward**.

aggravate/irritate

See Chapter 1, page 14.

agnostic/atheist

See **atheist/agnostic** on page 205.

aisle/isle

These words are homophones. They have nothing in common except their pronunciation and the fact that they are both quite short, and yet people frequently muddle them up. **Aisle** refers to a passage between rows of seats in a church, theatre, train, plane, etc, or the passageway between display shelving in supermarkets, as in:

> *The bride was about to walk down the aisle.*

> *She pushed her trolley down several of the aisles looking for cans of dog food.*

The word **isle** means 'island' and is frequently found in place names such as the *Isle of Wight* or the *Isle of Skye*. Otherwise it is mostly found in literary contexts.

all right/alright

There is a considerable dispute going on over the spelling of this word. On the one hand we have many, many people who are in the **all right** camp. They learnt from childhood that **all right** is the correct form and that is it as far as they are concerned. They are outraged that the spelling **alright** should even be mentioned. However, in the other camp are quite a few people, especially young people, who do not seem to realize that there is anything wrong with **alright** and that is the way they spell it.

Who is right? Well, at the moment the traditionalists are. **All right** is the only spelling that is considered correct, but all that could change, particularly in informal contexts.

Why has the dispute occurred? Well, it probably has something to do with words such as **already** and **altogether**. Some people think that **all right** should be used to indicate that something is completely correct but that **alright** can be used to mean 'acceptable' or 'satisfactory'. But they are wrong – at least for the time being!

alter/altar

Of these two homophones **alter** is by far the more common. It is a verb meaning 'to change', as in:

> *I need to alter this dress slightly.*

> *They're going to alter the times of the trains from next week.*

Alter is frequently confused with **altar**, a noun common in religious contexts and used in the Christian church to mean the table on which the bread and wine are blessed in communion services, as in:

> *The priest stood before the altar.*

Altar can also be used to refer to a table or other place where formerly sacrifices were offered to a god, as in:

> *The lamb was killed and put on the altar as an*
> *offering to the gods.*

altogether/all together

It is very easy to confuse these words. **Altogether** can mean
'completely', as in:

> *I can't say I'm altogether happy with the situation.*

It can also mean 'all in all', as in:

> *The rooms were comfortable, the food was good, the*
> *staff were polite and altogether it was an excellent*
> *hotel.*

All together means 'at the same time' or 'in the same place', as in:

> *It is the first Christmas for many years that we have*
> *been all together as a family.*

alternate/alternative

In British English **alternative** is an adjective which suggests the
offer of a choice of a second possibility, as in:

> *The road is closed but the police have suggested an*
> *alternative route.*

In American English **alternate** is often used in this context
instead of **alternative**. To some extent the American use of
alternate in this context is now found in British English also,
although **alternative** remains the common British form.

This should not be confused with **alternate** meaning 'every
other', as in:

> *We meet for lunch on alternate Saturdays.*

Nor should it be confused with **alternate** meaning 'happening in
turns, one after the other', as in:

> *The cake has alternate layers of cream and jam.*

amiable/amicable

Both of these adjectives can mean 'friendly' but they are not
interchangeable.

Amiable is usually used of people to mean friendly, pleasant and likeable, as in:

> *He was an amiable young man and all his fellow*
> *workers got on with him.*

Amicable is usually used to describe friendly relationships or dealings with other people, as in:

> *I think that husband and wife had both grown tired*
> *of each other but their separation seems to have*
> *been quite an amicable affair.*

among/between
The prepositions **among** and **between** may be used interchangeably in most contexts. Formerly **among** was used when referring to three or more people or things, as in:

> *We divided the remaining food among the five children.*

Between was used only when referring to two people or things, as in:

> *Sue's parents divided the money between her and*
> *her brother.*

In modern usage, however, **between** is often used when referring to more than two things (although some people object to this use), as in:

> *An agreement has been reached between all the*
> *states of America.*

any more/anymore
This term meaning 'any longer' is often spelt as one word in American English, and usually as two words in British English, as in:

> *She's giving these clothes away because she doesn't*
> *wear them any more.*

However, the American way of spelling is spreading to British English and becoming more and more common.

anyone/any one

Anyone is spelt as one word when it means the same as **anybody**, as in:

> *Anyone can succeed in this industry if they work hard enough.*

Anyone is used with a singular verb. In modern usage it is sometimes followed by a plural personal pronoun or plural possessive adjective to avoid sexism, as in:

> *Has anyone parked their car in the courtyard?*

Any one is spelt as two words in contexts such as:

> *Any one of those dresses would suit you.*

> *Any one of those college courses would be interesting.*

any place/anyplace

Formerly in British English the term **any place** was always written as two words and it was considered to be less acceptable, especially in formal contexts, than **anywhere**, as in:

> *We can't find any place to stay tonight.*

> *There are no hotels with vacancies any place in this area.*

The expression is much less common and more informal in British English than in American English. In American English the expression is often spelt as one word, **anyplace**, and this use is, to some extent, now spreading to British English.

any time/anytime

Formerly in British English the expression **any time** was always written as two words, as in:

> *Please come and see us any time.*

In American English, however, the expression is often spelt as one word, **anytime**, and this use is spreading to British English.

arbiter/arbitrator
See **A miscellany of mistakes** on page 191.

atheist/agnostic
These words do not mean the same but they both relate to the same theme, a belief, or rather a non-belief, in God. An **atheist** is someone who does not believe in the existence of God, as in:

> *My brother is marrying the daughter of a Church of England minister, although he himself is an atheist.*

An **agnostic** is not quite so certain, being someone who believes that it is impossible to know whether God exists or not. However, the word is used in a more general sense to refer to someone who doubts that God exists, as in:

> *He says that scientists deal in facts and as a result many of them are agnostics.*

aural/oral *see* oral/aural

averse/adverse *see* adverse/averse

backward/backwards
In British English **backward** is normally used as an adjective, as in:

> *She turned away and left without a backward glance.*

The word **backwards** is usually an adverb, as in:

> *He stepped backwards to get away from the heat of the bonfire.*

In American English **backward** is used as an adverb, as in:

> *He moved backward into the shadow of the building.*

balk/baulk
Both these spellings of this verb meaning 'to stop short of' or 'to recoil from' are acceptable, as in:

> *We balked/baulked at the idea of paying so much money for theatre tickets.*

bated/baited
In the expression with bated breath meaning 'to hold one's breath in fear or suspense' you wait with **bated** not **baited** breath, as in:

> *We waited with bated breath for the judges to announce the winner of the competition.*

bathroom
In British English a **bathroom** is usually a room containing a bath. In American English **bathroom** is often used as the word for a **toilet** or **lavatory** and this use is now sometimes found in British English. *See* **toilet/loo/lavatory** on page 246.

because of/due to/owing to
See Chapter 4, page 72.

beat/beaten
These parts of the verb beat are liable to be confused. The word **beat** is the past tense of the verb beat, as in:

> *They beat the defending champions easily.*

The word **beaten** is used as the past participle, as in:

> *They have beaten last year's champions.*

See Chapter 7, page 162.

bill/bill
See **Homonyms** on page 189.

black
See Chapter 6, page 151–52.

bow/bow
These words are homographs. They are spelt the same but pronounced differently and have totally different meanings. One rhymes with *low* and *mow* and means, among other things, 'a looped knot', as in:

> *She tied her daughter's hair ribbon in a bow.*

The other rhymes with *cow* and *how* and means the bending of the upper body as a mark of respect, as in:

He sang two songs, gave a quick bow and left the stage.

bridal/bridle

These words are homophones, being pronounced in the same way but with different spelling and different meanings. **Bridal** is an adjective meaning 'relating to a bride or to a wedding', as in:

The bridal car was decorated with white ribbons.

The word **bridle** refers to a harness for a horse's head, as in:

He bought a new bridle for his horse.

brooch/broach

These words are also homophones, being pronounced in the same way but with different spelling and different meanings.

Brooch is the commoner of the two words and is a noun referring to a piece of jewellery that is pinned to a garment, as in:

She wore a beautiful diamond brooch in the lapel of her jacket.

Broach is a verb meaning 'to introduce or mention a subject', as in:

He didn't like to broach the subject of the money she owed him.

calf/calf

See page 189.

canvas/canvass

These words are spelt slightly differently but are pronounced in the same way.

Canvas is a noun that refers to a kind of heavy coarse cloth that is used to make tents, etc, and also used by artists to paint on.

Canvass is a verb meaning 'to try to get people's votes in an election of some kind' as in *politicians canvassing for votes.*

can/may

The verb **can** is used to indicate either that someone or something is able to do something, as in:

He can ski but not very well.

The verb **may** can be used to indicate what is likely or possible, as in:

> *He may or may not attend the meeting – it depends on his other engagements.*

So far so good. The problem is that both **may** and **can** are now used to mean 'permitted or allowed to', as in:

> *You may/can go to the party if you are back home by 11 pm.*

Language purists who do not like language to change dislike **can** being used in this way, but they have lost the battle. For in all but the most formal contexts **can** is now the usual word in this context, as in:

> *Can I go now?*

You will still find **may** being used when people are being exceptionally polite, as in:

> *How may I help you, sir?*

censor/censure
These words are closely related and liable to be confused.

Censor can be a verb meaning 'to examine letters, publications, films, etc, and remove any material that is thought to be unsuitable in the circumstances', as in:

> *They censored the soldiers' letters in case they mentioned information that would be useful to the enemy.*

Censor can also be a noun used to refer to someone who censors something, as in:

> *He was employed as a censor of soldiers' letters.*

Censure can also act both as a verb and as a noun. As a verb it means 'to criticize or blame someone for something', as in:

> *The young lawyer was censured for his poor handling of the case.*

As a noun **censure** means 'severe criticism or blame', as in:

> *The government received censure for their*
> *unsuccessful economic policy.*

centenary/centennial

Both of these words refer to a hundred-year anniversary.
Centenary is the usual British English word, as in:

> *We are celebrating the centenary of the local*
> *school.*

Centennial is used more frequently in American English.

cheque/check

Both of these words mean 'an order to a bank to pay money from a person's account'. **Cheque** is the accepted form in British English, as in:

> *I don't have enough cash with me so I'll have to pay*
> *the bill by cheque.*

Check is the accepted American form. Nowadays paying by cheque is on the way out as it has largely been replaced with paying by credit or debit card.

chronic/acute

See page 194.

city/town

Nowadays a **city** is just a place that is larger and more important than a town, as in:

> *Usually I just shop for new clothes here in the town,*
> *but if I want something special I go to one of the*
> *larger shops in the city.*

In Britain the right for a town to be called a city is granted by the king or queen, although it is widely assumed that a town has to have a cathedral before it can be called a city. Many cities do have cathedrals, but this is not essential.

coloured

See Chapter 6, page 151.

complimentary/complementary

Complimentary is an adjective expressing admiration or praise, as in:

She was flattered by his complimentary remarks.

When connected with the giving of tickets, products etc, it is often used to mean 'given free', as in:

Each copy of the magazine has a complimentary diary inside it.

Complementary is an adjective referring to things that form a useful or attractive combination, although they may be quite different, as in:

She was careful to put together a team of people who had complementary skills.

In modern usage **complementary** is commonly found in the term **complementary medicine**, which uses treatments that are not part of the usual scientific Western medical methods. The term emphasizes the fact that its treatments coexist with scientific treatments, rather than replacing them, as is the case with **alternative medicine**.

comprehensible/comprehensive

These two adjectives are both derived from the verb **comprehend**, but they are not derived from the same sense of that verb. **Comprehensible** means 'able to be understood' as in:

The child is just learning to speak and what she's saying is only comprehensible to her mother.

It is often found in the negative form **incomprehensible,** as in:

Why he suddenly decided to give up such a good job is completely incomprehensible.

Comprehensive means 'including all or most things', as in:

You would be wise to take out fully comprehensive car insurance.

compulsory/compulsive

See page 192.

contagious/infectious

Both these words are adjectives referring to diseases that can be passed on from the sufferer to other people. **Contagious** diseases are passed on by direct physical contact, as in:

> *He has been told not to attend school as he*
> *is suffering from a skin disease that is highly*
> *contagious.*

Infectious diseases are passed on by airborne microorganisms, as in:

> *Some infectious diseases, such as measles and mumps,*
> *are now much rarer as a result of vaccination.*

continual/continuous

See page 190.

credible/credulous/incredible

These adjectives refer to belief but they are quite different in meaning. If something is **credible** it is believable, as in:

> *Both their accounts of what had happened sounded*
> *quite credible, but one of them must have been*
> *lying.*

Credulous is used of someone who is too ready to believe that whatever they are told is true, as in:

> *Only someone as credulous as Tom would believe*
> *that a car as cheap as that would be in good*
> *condition.*

It is very common now for people to use **credulous** when they really mean **credible**.

The opposite of **credible** is **incredible**, as in:

> *It seems incredible that no one stopped to help the*
> *injured man.*

criteria/criterion

People often use **criteria** wrongly as a singular noun but **criterion** is the singular form, as in:

> *A good degree is not the only criterion for selecting someone for the job.*

Criteria is the plural form, as in:

> *He meets all the basic criteria for the job but let's see how he does in his interview.*

cue/queue

Visually these two nouns do not resemble each other at all. However, they are pronounced in the same way to rhyme with *mew* and *dew*.

Cue has two quite different meanings. In sport it can mean a kind of stick used in billiards. In the theatre it can refer to a few words or an action that is a signal for another actor to do or say something:

> *He stood waiting for his cue to go on stage.*

Forming a **queue** is something the British are traditionally famous for, although I am not sure we are quite so disciplined as we used to be. A **queue** is line of people waiting in an orderly way to buy something, get into a building, etc, as in:

> *There was a huge queue outside the shop for the opening day of their sale.*

Queue can also act as a verb, as in:

> *We had to queue for more than an hour to get into the pop concert.*

currant/current

See **Homophones** on page 185.

deceitful/deceptive

Both of these adjectives are connected with deceiving or misleading someone. **Deceitful** is used of people or their words or actions when these are intended to deceive or mislead someone, as in:

> *She has always been a very deceitful person and*
> *it was typical of her not to tell her fiancé the truth*
> *about her background.*

Deceptive is used to describe things that are likely to mislead people, although there may be no dishonest intention involved, as in:

> *The cottage looks deceptively small on*
> *the outside – it's actually very spacious inside.*

delusion/illusion

These two words are liable to be confused because they are very close in meaning. **Delusion** refers to a false or mistaken belief or idea that someone holds about themselves or their situation, as in:

> *He is under the delusion that she has fallen in love*
> *with him.*

Sometimes such an idea or belief can be part of a mental disorder, as in:

> *She suffers from the delusion that she is Joan of*
> *Arc.*

Illusion refers to something that appears to be the case, but is not, as in:

> *The mountains seemed to be very close but it was*
> *an optical illusion.*

dependant/dependent

The noun **dependant** refers to a person who depends on someone else to supply their means of living, as in:

> *He said that he would resign from his job tomorrow*
> *if he could but he has dependants.*

The word **dependent** is an adjective meaning 'relying on' or 'unable to do without', as in:

> *She can't drive any more and she is dependent*

on her neighbour taking her for her hospital appointments.

Dependent often means 'relying on someone for financial support', as in:

He has no dependent relatives.

Note that in American English both the noun and adjective are spelt **dependent**.

deprecate/depreciate

These words look quite alike and they are liable to be confused. The word **deprecate** means 'to feel or express deep disapproval of', 'to deplore' or 'to condemn', as in:

The speaker deprecated the government's attitude to asylum speakers, describing their latest proposals as inhuman and totally lacking in compassion or sensitivity.

The verb **depreciate** can mean 'to decrease in value', as in:

Shares in the company have depreciated to an all-time low.

The verb **depreciate** can also mean 'to belittle or treat as insignificant', as in:

He was doing his best to speak French, but the teacher depreciated his efforts in front of the rest of the class.

It is this second meaning of **depreciate** that has become confused with that of **deprecate** and the two are now often used interchangeably, although language purists remain opposed to this. The change began with the adjective **self-deprecating**, which means 'modest or playing down your own achievements', as in *he is very self-deprecating.*

derisory/derisive

The adjective **derisory** is normally used in the sense of 'ridiculously small' or 'inadequate', as in:

> *The workers say that they have been offered a*
> *derisory pay rise and they are planning to go on strike.*

The adjective **derisive** means 'mocking', as in:

> *The comedian's act was not at all funny and was*
> *greeted with derisive comments from members of*
> *the audience.*

desert/dessert

Desert has the emphasis on the first syllable and, as a noun, it refers to an area of land that is very hot and dry, as in *the Sahara Desert*. As a verb **desert** has the stress on the second syllable and means 'to abandon someone or something', as in:

> *She deserted me when we were out together so I*
> *had to go home alone.*

The noun **dessert** has the emphasis on the second syllable and it means the last, sweet course of a meal, as in:

> *The children all want ice cream for dessert.*

device/devise

These words look and sound quite alike but they are entirely different in meaning. **Device** is a noun pronounced to rhyme with *advice* and means a tool or gadget, as in:

> *Do you have one of those devices for taking the*
> *corks out of wine bottles?*

Devise is a verb pronounced to rhyme with *advise* and means 'to invent or put together', as in:

> *The prisoners of war devised a clever escape plan.*

disc/disk

These words are liable to cause confusion because of the influence of American English. In British English the correct spelling is **disc**, as in:

> *He is suffering from a slipped disc and his back is*
> *very sore.*

But when the word is associated with computers it becomes **disk**, as in *disk drive*. In American English the word is generally spelt **disk** whatever the meaning. Many British English users are beginning to follow suit. *See* also Chapter 1, page 20.

discreet/discrete

These adjectives are pronounced the same but spelt differently and so are homophones. **Discreet** is often misspelt as **discrete**. The word **discreet** is the more common of the two words and, when used of a person, means 'careful not to tell secrets' or 'careful not to offend or embarrass people', as in:

> *You can safely confide in my mother because she's very discreet and won't tell anyone else about your problem.*

When used of behaviour or actions **discreet** means 'tactful' or 'careful to avoid attention', as in:

> *Thanks to her discreet handling of the situation, the affair was not made public.*

Discrete is a much less common, often technical, adjective meaning 'separate' or 'distinct', as in *discrete particles of the mineral.*

disinterested/uninterested

See Chapter 1, page 14.

downward/downwards

In British English **downward** is normally used as an adjective, as in:

> *The downward escalator is at the back of the store.*

Downwards is used as an adverb in British English, as in:

> *He took a few steps downwards from the summit and slipped.*

In American English **downward** is frequently used as an adverb.

drunk/drunken

These words are connected with alcoholic intoxication, but they are not used interchangeably. The adjective **drunk** is often used after a verb, as in:

> *The teenagers got very drunk on cheap cider.*

It often refers to a temporary state of intoxication.

Drunk can also be used as a noun to describe someone who drinks a lot of alcohol and is often drunk, as in:

> *The old drunk stopped me and asked for money.*

The adjective **drunken** is used before a noun, as in:

> *He was suffering from a hangover after a drunken party.*

Drunken is often used to describe someone who is in the habit of drinking too much and becoming intoxicated, as in:

> *The family never have any money because their drunken father spends all he earns on alcohol.*

due to/because of/owing to
See Chapter 4, page 72.

each and everyone
See Chapter 1, page 28.

economic/economical
Economic is an adjective referring to the economy or to economics, as in:

> *I wouldn't open a new business in the present economic climate.*

Economical is an adjective meaning 'concerned with using the minimum of resources and avoiding waste', as in:

> *He's looking for a small car that's economical to run.*

effect/affect *see* **affect/effect**

e.g./i.e.
These abbreviations refer to quite different things but they are

frequently confused, perhaps because not very many people learn Latin at school any more. The abbreviation **e.g.** means 'for example' and is short for the Latin expression *exempli gratia*. The abbreviation **e.g.** is used in such contexts as:

> *There are many historical places to visit in London,*
> *e.g. the Tower of London and the Natural History*
> *Museum.*

The abbreviation **i.e.** is short for the Latin expression *id est* and means 'that is'. It is used to introduce a brief explanation or amplification of what has just been said, as in:

> *Before we set up business in here we need to get*
> *some office equipment, i.e. a computer, a printer*
> *and some desks.*

Originally both of these abbreviations were spelt with full stops, but they are now frequently spelt without them in British English, as in eg and ie.

elder/older

Elder and **older** are both adjectives relating to age comparison and are sometimes confused. The word **elder** is used only in comparing the ages of people within a group, often a family group, as in:

> *John was Anne's elder brother.*

> *Aunt Jane was my mother's elder sister.*

You can also say:

> *She was the elder of my mother's two sisters.*

Elder cannot be followed by **than**. **Older** can be used instead of **elder** but it can also be used of things as well as people, as in:

> *I prefer older houses.*

Older can be followed by **than**, as in:

> *Their car is even older than mine.*

enquiry/inquiry

The words **enquiry** and **inquiry** can be used interchangeably in British English, although **inquiry** is the standard form in American English. Some people, however, prefer to use **enquiry** in British English to refer to an ordinary request for information, as in

> *One of the library staff will deal with your enquiry.*

Inquiry is used for a formal investigation of some kind, as in:

> *Police are interviewing him as part of a murder inquiry.*

envelope/envelop

These words look quite alike but they are pronounced differently and they have different meanings. The emphasis is on the first syllable of the noun **envelope**, which is a folded paper container in which you send a letter or card, as in:

> *I need an envelope for this birthday card.*

The emphasis is on the second syllable of **envelop**, which is a verb meaning 'to enclose or surround', as in:

> *The grandmother enveloped her grandson in a big hug.*

Note that the past tense and present participle of the verb **envelop** are spelt with a single *p*, as in **enveloped** and **enveloping**.

–ess

See Chapter 6, page 144.

every day/everyday

When this expression is used to mean 'daily' it is spelt as two words, as in:

> *She goes to the gym at least once every day.*

It is spelt as one word when it is used as an adjective to mean 'completely ordinary', as in:

> *It's a nice enough everyday dress but I want something special to wear for the wedding.*

Perhaps under the influence of such expressions as **any more/ anymore**, the distinction between **every day** and **everyday** is beginning to fade slightly and **everyday** is beginning to be used for both meanings. However, there is quite a long way to go before this is declared correct and acceptable and it will meet many protests along the way.

everyone/everybody/no one
See Chapter 1, page 29.

extant/extinct
The adjectives **extant** and **extinct** are opposites. **Extant** means 'still in existence', as in:

> *These are some of the traditions extant in the area around here.*

Extinct means 'no longer in existence', as in:

> *There are quite a few theories about why dinosaurs became extinct.*

extrovert/extravert/introvert
Extravert is the original spelling but **extrovert** is now the more common spelling.

Extrovert refers to someone who is more concerned with what is going on around them than with their own thoughts and feelings, and more particularly someone who is lively, confident and sociable, as in:

> *Our first two guests are both extroverts so they should get the party off to a good start.*

The opposite is **introvert** which refers to someone who is preoccupied with their own thoughts and feelings, particularly someone who is withdrawn and unsociable, as in:

> *He's an introvert who prefers his own company to that of other people.*

farther/further
Both **farther** and **further** can be used to refer to physical distance, as in:

> *The hotel is much farther from the city centre than we were told.*

> *My house is a bit further down this road.*

However, only **further** is used in other senses, as in:

> *The police officer said that he would take no further questions from members of the press.*

The verb form is also always **further**, as in:

> *The rebels vowed to further the cause of freedom.*

female/lady/woman
See **lady/woman/female** in Chapter 6, page 145.

female as a noun
See **female as a noun** in Chapter 6, page 146.

fewer/less
Fewer, the comparative form of **few**, means 'a smaller number of', as in:

> *Fewer students than usual have signed up for this course.*

Less, the comparative form of **little**, means 'a smaller amount than', as in:

> *Tell the children to make less noise.*

It is becoming common, especially in informal contexts, to use **less** in many cases where **fewer** is correct, although this use is ungrammatical and should be avoided in formal contexts.

first/firstly
When mentioning items in a list the first item may be preceded by either **firstly** or **first**, as in:

> *There are several reasons for my refusal to go: firstly/first I am much too busy to attend …*

Formerly **firstly** was considered unacceptable in this context.

flu
Formerly this word was preceded by an apostrophe and spelt **'flu**.

This was to show that the word is a shortened form of **influenza**, but the apostrophe is no longer commonly used. The long form, **influenza**, is only used in very formal or technical contexts.

forbear/forebear

The verb **forbear** is pronounced with the stress on the second syllable and it means 'to refrain from doing something'. It is mostly used in formal contexts, as in:

> *I shall forbear from punishing the students in the circumstances.*

The noun **forebear** is pronounced with the stress on the first syllable and can also be spelt **forbear**. It is used to refer to an ancestor, as in:

> *Some of our forebears probably lived in these ruins.*

for ever/forever

The two-word version of this expression is often used to emphasize that something is for all time, as in:

> *He said he would love her for ever.*

In the sense of 'continually or without stopping' the expression is usually written as one word, as in:

> *The child is forever asking for sweets.*

fortuitous/fortunate

See Chapter 1, page 17.

forward/forwards

In British English **forward** is used as an adjective, as in *a forward motion* and *some forward planning is required*. **Forward** and **forwards** can be used as adverbs, meaning 'towards the front', as in *step forward* and *move forwards*. However, in idiomatic phrasal verbs such as *put forward a motion* and *asking witnesses to come forward,* the word **forwards** is not used.

gaol/jail *see* jail/gaol

gay

See Chapter 1, page 15.

gipsy/gypsy
Both these spellings are acceptable, although some people object to this word however it is spelt, regarding it as offensive. It is accepted by some when spelt with a capital as in **Gypsy**. An alternative word is **Traveller**, although this is often used to refer to a wider range of people than Gypsies who are Romany in origin, including, for example, *Irish Travellers*. The approved modern alternative preferred by many in Europe is **Roma**.

girl
See Chapter 6, page 147.

gorilla/guerrilla *see* **guerrilla/guerilla/gorilla**

got/gotten
See page 196.

gourmet, gourmand
These two words are sometimes confused. They are both connected with food, but the word **gourmet** is a complimentary term used to describe someone who likes food and who is knowledgeable about it.

A **gourmand** also likes food, but is concerned with the amount of it that can be eaten, rather than with the quality of it. **Gourmand** means much the same as **glutton**, but does not sound so insulting!

guerrilla/guerilla/gorilla
These words are often pronounced in the same way although they are spelt quite differently and have completely different meanings.

Guerrilla, which has the alternative spelling **guerilla**, means a member of a small unofficial group of fighters, as in:

> *The soldiers were set upon by a band of guerrillas in the mountain pass.*

Gorilla is the name for the largest of the apes native to central Africa, as in:

> *The habitat of some gorilla species is being destroyed.*

gypsy/gipsy *see* **gipsy/gypsy**

hanged/hung
See page 196.

heal/heel
See page 185.

he and him
See Chapter 1, page 30.

hear/here
See page 186.

hire/rent
See page 195.

his and their
See Chapter 1, page 29.

historic/historical
See Chapter 1, page 16.

hoard/horde
These words are homophones since they sound alike but have different meanings. **Hoard** is a noun meaning 'a store or collection of something', as in:

> *She was supposed to be on a strict diet but she kept a hoard of chocolate bars in her bedroom.*

Horde is a disapproving word used to refer to a very large group of people, as in:

> *The resort is a restful place in the winter but hordes of tourists flock to it in the summer.*

holiday/vacation *see* **vacation/holiday**

hung/hanged *see* **hanged/hung**

hyper–/hypo–
These prefixes are liable to be confused. Although they sound similar they are opposite in meaning.

Hyper– means 'above', 'over,' or 'in excess', as in:

The child was said to be hyperactive.

Hypo– means 'under', 'beneath', as in:

She has to inject insulin with a hypodermic syringe.

Hypothermia is a medical condition in which the body temperature is much lower than normal.

i.e./e.g. *see* e.g./i.e.

illegible/eligible

These two words are liable to be confused, mainly because they sound similar, but they have entirely different meanings.

Illegible means 'impossible to read', as in:

I hope he types the information I asked for because his handwriting is virtually illegible.

Eligible means 'suitable' or 'having the right qualifications', as in:

She was pleased to find out that she was eligible for a scholarship.

illusion/delusion *see* delusion/illusion

immigrant/emigrant

These words are liable to be confused. This is quite understandable as the two words can refer to the same person, looked at from two different viewpoints. The word immigrant concentrates on people arriving in a new land, as in:

There were many Irish immigrants in America following the potato famine in Ireland.

The word emigrant concentrates on people leaving their native land, as in:

Many of the Irish people who left their native shore were reluctant emigrants, but they travelled to Britain and America to avoid starvation.

immoral/immortal
See page 193.

imply/infer
Imply means 'to suggest something in an indirect way', as in:

> *He didn't actually accuse the student of cheating outright, but he implied it.*

Infer means 'to deduce something' or 'to conclude that something is true', as in:

> *We inferred from the report that the hospital was almost certain to close.*

Nowadays **infer** is often used when the correct word is **imply**, as in:

> *He inferred that he would be leaving the job shortly.*

This is incorrect and should read:

> *He implied that he would be leaving the job shortly.*

impracticable/impractical/practicable/practical
The words **impracticable** and **impractical** are similar in meaning, but they are not interchangeable.

Impracticable means 'not able to be put into practice' or 'unworkable', as in:

> *He persuaded several people that the scheme was a good idea but it was so expensive that it was completely impracticable.*

Impractical means 'not sensible' or 'unrealistic', as in:

> *He has come up with various money-making ideas but all of them are impractical.*

Practicable and **practical** are the positive forms of these words, as in:

> *Do you think it is practicable to build a house halfway up a mountain?*

A two-seater car like that's not very practical when you have two children.

indexes/indices

The noun **index** has two possible plural forms, **indexes** and **indices**. The word **indexes** is the usual plural form in most contexts, as in:

Her job is to compile indexes for reference books.

The word **indices** is mostly restricted to technical or mathematical contexts.

individual

The word **individual** means 'a person', but it can only be used in certain contexts. **Individual** is often used in a context in which a single person is contrasted with a group, as in:

We must give some thought to the rights of the individual as well as concerning ourselves with the nation as a whole.

The word **individual** is sometimes used in a derogatory or insulting way, as in:

She was very nice but I always thought her husband was a most unpleasant individual.

industrial/industrious
See page 192.

infectious/contagious *see* contagious/infectious

infer/imply *see* imply/infer

inflammable/flammable/non-flammable
The two words inflammable and flammable both mean 'capable of burning' or 'easily set on fire', as in:

Children's nightclothes should not be made of inflammable/flammable material.

It is a common error to think that **inflammable** means the opposite, i.e. 'not capable of burning', because **in–** words, are often negative, as in *incredible,* but the word for this is **non-flammable**.

ingenious/ingenuous

These words are frequently confused although they are neither spelt the same way nor pronounced the same way and their meanings are entirely different. The **e** of the word **ingenious** is pronounced like the double **e** in the word *seen,* while the **e** of the word **ingenuous** is pronounced like the **e** in the word *egg.*

As to meaning, **ingenious** means 'clever, especially in an inventive or unusual way', as in:

> *She's a brilliant cook and finds a great many ingenious ways to use up leftover food.*

Ingenuous means naïve or innocent, as in:

> *His latest girlfriend is very young and too ingenuous to realize that he is a real womanizer.*

–ise/–ize *see* –ize/–ise

isle/aisle *see* aisle/isle

its/it's

These two little words are among the most often confused. **Its** is the possessive form of **it** and so it is used in such contexts as:

> *The dog has injured its paw.*

> *The holiday resort has lost its appeal for them.*

Note that **its** in this context does not have an apostrophe although an apostrophe is often used to show possession.

However, there is an apostrophe in **it's**, which is a contraction of **it is**, as in:

> *It's (it is) difficult to find a decent restaurant around here.*

> *It's (it is) getting late and it's (it is) time I was getting home.*

–ize/–ise

Either of these verb endings is correct in British English, with a few exceptions. In American English the **–ize** ending is the standard spelling and many British English dictionaries and reference books also use this spelling.

However, as long as British English users are consistent in their use of **–ize** or **–ise** it usually does not matter which they use. Note that there are some words in British English where the **–ize** spelling should not be used. These include *advertise*, *advise*, *chastise*, *comprise*, *compromise*, *exercise*, *improvise*, *revise*, *supervise*, *surmise*, *surprise* and *televise*.

jail/gaol
Both of these are acceptable spellings of the word for '*prison*', although **jail** is the more common spelling.

jewellery/jewelry
Both of these are acceptable spellings in British English, although **jewellery** is the more common spelling. In American English **jewelry** is the standard spelling.

judgement/judgment
Both of these forms are considered acceptable. **Judgement** is more common in British English, and **judgment** is more common in American English.

lady/woman/female
See Chapter 6, page 145.

lay/lie
These words can cause confusion. Not only are their meanings related, but the past tense of the word **lie** is **lay**. This is, indeed, a recipe for confusion!

The verb **lay** takes a direct object and means 'to put or place something down', as in:

> *The doctor asked them to lay the injured man on the stretcher.*

The verb **lie**, which gets confused with the verb **lay**, does not take a direct object and means 'to rest on something in a horizontal position', as in:

> *I feel faint and need to lie on the sofa.*

The past tense of **lay** is **laid**, as in:

We laid the baby on the bed.

The past tense of **lie** in this context is **lay**, as in:

He lay on the bed, groaning with pain.

The past participle of **lay** is **laid**, as in:

We had laid the baby on the bed.

The past participle of **lie** is **lain**, as in:

The lion had lain in wait unnoticed by its prey.

Just to add more confusion, there is another verb **to lie** which means 'to tell untruths'. Fortunately, neither its past tense nor its past participle causes any problems, both being formed regularly as **lied**.

lead/lead
See page 187.

learn/teach
The word **learn** is sometimes used wrongly instead of **teach**. If you are giving information or instruction about something to someone you **teach** them, as in:

She teaches English to Spanish students.

When you are gaining information or knowledge or getting instruction about something you **learn** something, as in:

*The French student has gone to live with a family
in London in order to learn English.*

lend/loan
The word **lend** is used as a verb and means 'to give someone the temporary use of', as in:

*I'm sure he'll lend you the book which you need for
your homework assignment.*

The verb **loan** is commonly used in American English in the above context, but in British English **loan** is mostly used with reference to the lending of reasonably large sums of money, valuable works of art, etc, as in:

> *The bank has agreed to loan us the money to start our new business.*

Lend is also commonly used in this context.

The word **loan** is also used as a noun, as in:

> *We have to repay the bank loan by the end of the year.*

It is not correct English to use **lend** as a noun, although some people do so in informal contexts.

less/fewer *see* fewer/less

libel/slander

Both **libel** and **slander** are nouns that refer to untrue statements intended to give people a bad opinion of someone.

In **libel** such statements are written down or printed, as in:

> *She is suing the newspaper on the grounds of libel since one of their reporters wrongly accused her of being drunk and disorderly in a night club.*

In **slander** the statements are spoken, as in:

> *She is guilty of slander if she told you that he deserted his wife and children. He's not even married.*

Both **libel** and **slander** can also be used as verbs.

licence/license

These words are often wrongly used. In British English **licence** is a noun, as in:

> *The police officer asked to see his driving licence.*

> *The shopkeeper has applied for a licence to sell alcohol.*

Note the spelling of **off-licence**, which is a noun referring to premises in the UK where you can buy bottles or cans of alcoholic drinks to take away.

License is a verb, as in:

> *The organizers of the event are not licensed to sell alcohol.*

The past participle form **licensed** is often used as an adjective, as in *licensed grocer* and *licensed restaurant* and this is often wrongly written as licenced. In American English things are simpler because both the noun and the verb are spelt **license**.

loan/lend *see* lend/loan

lose/loser/loose/looser

The words **lose** and **loose** are sometimes confused although they are neither spelt in the same way nor pronounced in the same way. **Lose** is spelt with only one *o* and is pronounced to rhyme with whose, while **loose** is spelt with double *o* and is pronounced to rhyme with goose.

Lose is a verb meaning 'to be unable to find something' as in:

> *If you lose your credit card you should ring your bank right away.*

It can also mean 'to fail to win', as in:

> *If you lose this match you'll be out of the competition.*

A **loser** is someone who fails to win, although it is often used to refer to someone who never seems to win or be successful in life in general, as in:

> *How did such a successful businesswoman come to marry such a loser?*

Loose is an adjective meaning 'not tight', as in:

> *She's lost some weight and her clothes are now a bit loose.*

If something is **looser** than it was before it is not so tight or close-fitting.

–man

See **Removing –man** in Chapter 6, page 141.

mankind
See **Is mankind no more?** in Chapter 6, page 143.

masterly/masterful
These adjectives are both derived from the noun **master** but they have different meanings.

Masterly means 'very skilful', as in:

> *The audience applauded a masterly performance*
> *by the orchestra.*

Masterful means 'showing strength or dominance', as in:

> *He thought he was being masterful, but she thought*
> *he was being a bully.*

metre/meter
These words are liable to be confused. In British English a **metre** is the basic metric measurement of length, being also used in such derived forms as *kilometre* and *millimetre*.

Meter is a measuring instrument, as in *gas meter, speedometer.* *Note that in American English both the measurement and the measuring instruments are spelt* **meter**.

migrant
A **migrant** is someone who travels from one place or country to another, often in order to try to find work, as in:

> *The farmer employed several migrants from*
> *eastern Europe.*

Migrant can also be used as an adjective, as in *migrant workers.* It is also used frequently to refer to birds travelling from place to place according to the season of the year, as in:

> *Swallows are migrants to Britain during the*
> *summer months.*

Migrant is liable to be confused with **immigrant** and **emigrant**. *See* **immigrant/emigrant** on page 226.

minute/minute
See page 188.

misuse/abuse *see* **abuse/misuse**

momentary/momentous

These two adjectives are both derived from the noun **moment**, but they are connected with different meanings of **moment**. The stress on **momentary** is on the first syllable and the stress on **momentous** is on the second syllable.

Momentary comes from the common 'time' meaning of **moment**, i.e. 'a very short time', and it means 'lasting a very short time', as in:

> *The chess player had a momentary failure of concentration, but then he began to play better than ever.*

Momentous comes from a less common meaning of **moment**, i.e. 'importance' or 'significance', and means 'very significant or having far-reaching consequences', as in:

> *It was a momentous decision to invade another country, and one that the president was to regret.*

moral/morale

Although these words are pronounced in different ways and have totally different meanings the fact that they look quite alike makes them easily confused.

Moral is most commonly an adjective and means 'referring to the principles of right and wrong', as in:

> *Their mother is a very moral person and yet both her sons are criminals.*

> *He had a moral responsibility to look after the children in his care.*

Moral as a noun is used to refer to a lesson on how to behave or act, often one which you learn from reading a story, as in:

> *There is often a moral in the stories from Aesop's Fables.*

Morale refers to how members of a group are feeling and the extent of their confidence and optimism, as in:

> *After their election victory, morale in the political
> party is at an all-time high.*

nauseous
See Chapter 1, page 18.

next/this
The adjective **next** in one of its senses is used to refer to the day of the week, the month of the year, etc, that will follow, as in:

> *I'll see you next Tuesday.*

The adjective **this** can also be used in this way and this can give rise to ambiguity. For example, some people use **this** to refer to the very next Tuesday, reserving **next** for the Tuesday after that. Others use **next** for both. In order to avoid this ambiguity it is best to specify exactly what day or date you are referring to.

non-flammable *see* **flammable/inflammable**

obscene/pornographic
These words are not interchangeable, although they are both often used of literature that is of a sexual nature and can give offence.

Obscene means connected with sex in a way that is considered indecent or offensive according to usual standards, as in:

> *The women were shocked by the obscene graffiti on
> the bus shelter.*

Obscene is now frequently used loosely to mean 'disgusting', 'repulsive' or 'abominable' in contexts that have nothing to do with sex, as in:

> *Some people feel that senior executives in banking
> sometimes earn an obscene amount of money.*

Pornographic is used of magazines, films, etc, that are intended to arouse sexual excitement, often by showing sexual acts and imagery which many people find offensive. Note the letter **c** in **obscene**. The word is often misspelt.

of/have
Of is sometimes used wrongly instead of the verb **have** in certain

contexts, perhaps because they sound rather alike when not emphasized or pronounced clearly. To write or say *should of come* instead of *should have come* or *must of done* instead of *must have done* is becoming more and more common but it is still considered wrong.

off/from

The word **off** is used by some people instead of **from** in certain contexts, for example when they wish to indicate where they acquired something, as in:

I certainly wouldn't buy a second-hand car off him.

This use is incorrect and should be avoided, especially in formal contexts.

off + of

Some people wrongly use **off** followed by **of** when only **off** is necessary, as in:

The cat jumped off of the table and ran out the door.

older/elder *see* elder/older

one/you *see* you/one

oral/aural

These words are liable to be confused. This is not surprising because they sound the same and they both refer to parts of the body involved in communication.

Aural means 'relating to the sense of hearing'. For example, in an *aural comprehension test* the test is read out to the students so that they have to understand it through hearing before answering the questions, usually in writing. The word **aural** can also refer to the ear, but usually only in technical or formal contexts.

Oral means 'referring to speech'. In an *oral test* the questions and answers are all spoken. **Oral** is also used to mean 'referring to the mouth', as in *oral hygiene*.

oral/verbal *see* verbal/oral

orientate/orient

Both of these forms are considered acceptable in British English in the sense of 'to get your bearings', although **orientate** is the more commonly used, as in:

> *The mist was coming down and it was becoming*
> *increasingly difficult to orientate themselves on the*
> *mountain slopes.*

In American English the standard form is **orient**.

outdoor/outdoors
These words refer to the same thing, but they are different parts of speech. **Outdoor** is used as an adjective, as in:

> *They try to persuade their children to get involved*
> *in outdoor sports at the weekend and during the*
> *holidays.*

Outdoors is used as an adverb, as in:

> *It's not often warm enough to eat outdoors in this*
> *climate.*

outward/outwards
These words both mean 'towards the outside', but they are not generally considered to be interchangeable in British English. **Outward** is used as an adjective, as in:

> *The train on the outward journey was very late,*
> *but it was on time on the way back.*

Outwards is used as an adverb, as in:

> *The dancers stood with their toes pointing*
> *outwards.*

In American English **outward** can be used both as an adjective and an adverb.

partner
See **Significant others** in Chapter 6, page 148.

passed/past
These words sound alike and are homophones which are liable to be confused.

The word **passed** is the past tense and past participle of the verb **pass**, as in:

We passed the school on our way here.

The word **past** can be a noun, as in:

You must try to forget the past.

It can be an adjective, as in:

He seems to have forgotten all about his past crimes.

Past can also act as a preposition, as in:

We must have driven past the church without noticing it.

It can be an adverb, as in:

I looked out of the window and saw them walking past.

person
See Chapter 6, page 144.

persecute/prosecute
See page 193.

phenomenon/phenomena
People often use **phenomena** wrongly as a singular noun when it is **phenomenon** that is the singular form, as in:

There have been many reports of the phenomenon that appeared in the sky last night but astronomers are still baffled by it.

pornographic/obscene *see* obscene/pornographic

practicable/practical *see* impracticable/impractical

practice/practise
These words are liable to be confused and used wrongly. **Practice** is a noun, as in:

He goes to football practice after school on Tuesdays.

Unfortunately our doctor has moved to a new practice in another town.

Some members of the company were involved in illegal practices.

Practise is the verb form, as in:

They practise playing the piano every day.

He is not qualified to practise medicine in this country.

Note that **practise** is not one of those verbs in English that can end in **–ize**. Note also that in American English both the noun and verb forms are spelt **practise**.

precede/proceed

These words are commonly confused. The word **precede** means 'to go or come in front of someone or something', as in:

The staff and sixth-year students preceded the rest of the school into the assembly hall.

The main text of the book was preceded by a short but informative introduction.

Who preceded David Cameron as prime minster of Britain?

The word **proceed** means 'to go on' or 'to continue', as in:

They did not proceed with the changes.

It also means 'to make your way' or 'to go', as in:

You should proceed to Gate 4 immediately.

prescribe/proscribe

Prescribe is the more common of these two words and means 'to advise' or 'order the use of', often in a medical context, as in:

> *The doctor prescribed a mild sleeping pill for the patient.*

> *He prescribed a few days of complete bed rest for my child.*

Proscribe is used in formal contexts to mean 'to forbid', as in:

> *The law proscribed the carrying of knives.*

principal/principle

These two words are pronounced in the same way but are spelt differently and have different meanings.

Principal as an adjective means 'chief or main', as in:

> *Her principal source of income is child-minding.*

> *Boredom was the principal reason for him leaving his job.*

Principal as a noun refers to the head or leader, as in:

> *The principal of the senior school met with the parents.*

Principle is a noun meaning 'a law', 'a basic principle' or 'a guiding rule', as in:

> *It was against her principles to eat meat.*

> *The research must be proved to conform with scientific principles.*

prostrate/prostate

These two words are often confused. **Prostrate** as an adjective means 'lying on the ground facing downwards', as in:

> *The victim of the attack was lying prostrate at the entrance to the park.*

It can also mean 'overcome' or 'shocked', as in:

> *She was prostrate with grief when she heard of her son's sudden death.*

Prostrate can also be a verb meaning 'to throw yourself on the ground, as in submission', as in:

> *They were obliged to prostrate themselves before the tyrannical president every morning.*

Prostate is a noun which refers to the gland round the neck of a man's bladder, as in:

> *He is being treated for prostate cancer.*

queer
See Chapter 1, page 16.

queue/cue *see* cue/queue

rain/reign/rein
See page 186.

rapt/wrapped
These words are sometimes confused because they sound alike. **Rapt** is an adjective meaning 'completely engrossed in something', as in:

> *The children watched with rapt attention while the magician performed his tricks.*

Wrapped is the past tense of the verb **wrap** meaning 'to enfold' or 'to cover', as in:

> *She wrapped the gift in tissue paper.*

It is the more figurative use of **wrapped** that is most likely to be confused with **rapt,** as in:

> *She was far too wrapped up in looking after her family to want to go out to work.*

–right/rite/write/wright
See page 186.

Scottish/Scots/Scotch

These adjectives all mean 'of or relating to Scotland'. However, they are not interchangeable. **Scottish** is the most general of these adjectives and it can be used in a wide range of contexts, as in:

> *Both her grandparents came from Scotland and she is very interested in Scottish culture.*

> *He paints watercolours of the Scottish landscape.*

The adjective **Scots** tends to be restricted to describing people, language or the law, as in *a dictionary of the Scots language* and in *Scots law.*

The noun **Scots** is used to refer to a person who comes from Scotland, as in:

> *Many Scots emigrated to Canada.*

The noun **Scots** is also used to refer to the Scots language, as in *writing in Scots*.

Scotch is the least general of the three adjectives, being restricted to a few contexts such as *Scotch broth*, *Scotch mist* and, the most famous of all, *Scotch whisky*. **Scotch** can also be used as a noun to mean '*Scotch whisky*', although this use is not common in Scotland where whisky is simply *whisky*.

seasonal/seasonable

These words are both adjectives formed from the noun **season**. **Seasonal** means 'relating to a particular season', 'occurring during a particular season' or 'varying with the seasons', as in:

> *The steak is served with seasonal vegetables.*

> *Farm work is usually seasonal in that area.*

Seasonable means 'suitable for or appropriate to a particular season', as in:

> *The weather this summer has not been very seasonable.*

shall/will *see* **will/shall**

stationary/stationery

These words sound alike and are often confused. The adjective **stationary** means 'standing still' or 'not moving', as in:

> *Because of the traffic jam there was a line of stationary vehicles along the entire length of the high street.*

The noun **stationery** refers to materials used in writing, such as paper, envelopes, pens, etc, as in:

> *The only shop that sells stationery here is the village shop and it has a very limited stock.*

An easy way to remember the difference between the words is to keep in mind that **stationery** is sold by a **stationer**, which, in common with words like **baker**, ends in **–er**.

swallow/swallow

See page 189.

swingeing/swinging

There are both spelling and pronunciation problems connected with swingeing, which means 'extensive and severe' and is often used in a financial context, as in:

> *Government ministers are proposing swingeing cuts in public spending.*

Note the letter *e* which differentiates the word from **swinging**, the present participle of the verb **swing**. **Swingeing**, unlike **swinging**, is pronounced *swin-jing*.

systematic/systemic

Both these adjectives are connected with the noun **system**. **Systematic** means 'well-organized and orderly', as in:

> *The police conducted a systematic search of the house and grounds.*

> *You need to establish a more systematic process for selecting new staff.*

Systemic refers to a system and is a much less common word sometimes used in error for **systematic**. **Systemic** is used mainly in scientific or medical contexts, as in:

> *Her illness began with an infected finger but it has developed into a serious systemic disease of the blood.*

that/which

That and **which** are both relative pronouns. **That** can be used to refer to people or things, as in:

> *There is the man that I was talking about.*

> *That pen was very expensive.*

Whereas **which** can only be used to refer to things or animals and not people, as in:

> *The cat, which I see every day, lives with John.*

That *and* **which** *are often used interchangeably as in:*

> *This is the cake that Mary made.*

> *This is the cake which Mary made.*

This is not necessarily considered wrong, however, there is a distinction to be made: **that** defines (it appears in a restrictive relative clause), and **which** gives extra information (it appears in a non-restrictive relative clause) and is usually preceded by a comma.

> *The cake, which Mary made for me, is damaged.*

> *The boy told me that he was Spanish, which is what I thought originally.*

The relative pronoun **who** can be used instead of **that** to refer to people:

> *That is the boy who told me he was Spanish.*

the
The is the definite article. It is sometimes pronounced *thee* when it is used to refer to someone or something that is unique or of great importance, as in:

> *You mean you've been on the* (thee) *Orient Express?*

Avoid using such expressions as **the poor** and **the old,** because it is insulting to lump people together in that way. It ignores the fact that they are individuals. Use **poor people** and **older people** instead.

their/they're
These words have similar pronunciations and are sometimes confused. **Their** is a possessive pronoun meaning 'belonging to or connected with them', as in:

> *They have parked their car at the station.*

They're is short for **they are,** as in:

> *They're here now.*

> *They're too young to learn to drive.*

there/their
The words **there** and **their** are sometimes confused. **There** means 'in that place', as in *just over there,* and in such contexts as:

> *There is an excellent library in the town.*

Their is a possessive pronoun meaning 'belonging to or connected with them', as in *their clothes* and *their kindness.*

this/next *see* **next/this**

to/too
These words are sometimes confused. The word **to** is used as a preposition, as in:

> *I'm going to the supermarket.*

To is also used with the infinitive of a verb, as in:

> *They want to leave.*

The word **too** can mean 'also' or 'as well', as in:

> *You can come too.*

Or it can mean 'excessively', as in:

> *This flat is far too expensive for us.*

toilet/loo/lavatory
Toilet is the most widely used of these words, although **loo** is becoming more and more widely used, especially in less formal situations. The word **lavatory** is more formal but not often used nowadays. **Toilet** is usually found on relevant signs in public places. There are many euphemisms for the word **toilet**, such as **rest room, smallest room, little boys'/little girls' room** etc. *See* **bathroom** on page 206.

toward/towards
These two forms of the preposition meaning 'in the direction of something or someone', 'close or closer to a point in time' or 'in relation to someone or something' are interchangeable except that in British English **towards** is the more common form, as in *walk towards them* and towards *the end of the week.*

In American English **toward** is the more common form, as in *coming toward us and toward the end of the week.*

town/city *see* city/town

try to/try and
These two expressions are often interchangeable in modern usage, as in:

> *Let's try to get this finished today.*

> *Let's try and get this finished today.*

Formerly **try and** was considered to be unacceptable in all but very informal or colloquial contexts, **try to** being the acceptable form. Now **try and** is acceptable in all but the most formal written contexts.

uninterested/disinterested *see* **disinterested/uninterested**

until/till
These words mean the same, but **until** tends to be used in more formal contexts and **till** is usually used in speech.

up/upon
These words mean the same, but **upon** tends to be used in more formal contexts.

upward/upwards
In British English **upward** is usually used as an adjective, as in *the upward escalator* and **upwards** as an adverb, as in *pointing upwards*. In American English **upward** is frequently used as an adverb.

vacation/holiday
In British English the word **holiday** is in general common use, as in:

> *They always go to France for their annual holiday.*

In American English the word **vacation** is used in this way, as in *their annual vacation*. In British English **vacation** is mostly used to refer to university and college holidays, as in:

> *Many students work in bars in their summer vacation.*

Vacation is sometimes used in British English in commercial contexts, as in:

> *We specialize in long-haul vacations.*

verbal/oral
There is a certain amount of ambiguity associated with the use of the word **verbal**. It can mean 'expressed in words' in writing and in speech, as in:

> *She made no verbal comment about the food although she looked at it with disgust.*

However, **verbal** is often used to refer to something that is spoken and not written down, as in:

Although we had a verbal agreement, we didn't put anything in writing.

If you are referring to something that is spoken rather than written, and if there is any possibility of ambiguity from the context, it is best to use the word **oral**, which can mean 'expressed in speech'. *See* **oral/aural.**

whisky/whiskey

Both refer to the strong alcoholic drink made from grain. The usual British English spelling is **whisky**, especially when this is made in Scotland. The Irish form of the drink is often spelt **whiskey**, and **whiskey** is the common American English spelling of both the Scottish and Irish drinks.

whom/who

The word **whom** is used as the object of a verb or preposition, as in:

Whom did he choose as his assistant?

To whom did he leave his house?

Whereas the word **who** is used as the subject, as in:

Who said that?

However, in modern usage **who** is increasingly being used instead of **whom** (except in very formal contexts) in situations where this is technically ungrammatical, as in:

Who did he choose as his assistant?

Who did he leave the house to?

whose/who's

These words sound alike and cause a good deal of confusion. The word **whose** means 'of whom' or 'of which', as in:

The employee whose wife has just had a baby has taken paternity leave.

Whose bike is this?

The word **who's** is short for **who is**, as in:

Who's giving the after-dinner speech?

Who's the woman wearing the bright red dress?

will/shall

The future tense of verbs is formed by using **will** or **shall**, or a contracted form of these, with the infinitive form of the main verb, as in:

The new shop will open for business next week.

We'll start work tomorrow.

Formerly, the verb **shall** was always used with *I* and *we* and **will** with *you*, *he/she/it* and *they*, as in:

I shall deliver the goods tomorrow.

She will start her duties next week.

There was an exception to this. **Will** was used with *I* and *we* and **shall** was used with the other personal pronouns when a firm intention was being expressed, as in:

Believe me, I will finish this in time.

My wife shall have that diamond necklace,
however much it costs.

In modern usage a change has occurred. The verb **will** is now commonly used in most contexts.

The word **shall** is sometimes used when questions are being asked or suggestions being made when these relate to the immediate situation, as in:

Shall I proceed?

Shall we get going?

In informal and relatively informal contexts the contracted form is used, as in:

Who'll go first?

What'll you have?

woman/lady/female
See **lady/woman/female** in Chapter 6, page 145.

wrapped/rapt *see* **rapt/wrapped**

you/one
Both of the pronouns you and one can be used to refer to an indefinite person or people in general. You is the pronoun you would use most often for this purpose, as in:

> *You need to book a seat when you buy your train ticket.*

> *You learn a foreign language more quickly if you spend some time in the country where it is spoken.*

> *You must buy a ticket before you board the train.*

The pronoun **one** was used formerly in these and other contexts, as in:

> *One must guard against pickpockets in the market.*

Now, however, **one** is usually restricted to very formal contexts, as in:

> *Etiquette demands that one must curtsey when being introduced to the Queen.*

your/you're
These words sound alike and they are commonly confused. The word **your** is a possessive pronoun meaning 'belonging to or connected with you', as in:

> *I forgot to give you your pen back.*

> *It was definitely your mistake.*

The word **you're** is short for **you are,** as in:

> *You're looking very cheerful today.*

> *You're really too ill to go to work today.*

9

PUTTING IT IN WRITING

Many of us use mobile phones to communicate with each other, whether this be for social or business purposes. When we do resort to using the written word this often takes the form of texting. Because of the small screen size on which texts are sent and received, texting tends to make great use of abbreviations, often based on the sound of individual letters and numbers. Thus B4 means 'before' and CU18r means 'see you later'.

There is a concern that texting is having an unfortunate effect on the spelling of some people who do not communicate very often in a more formal way, The truth is that fewer and fewer of us are regularly exchanging information by means of formal written communications. Here are some tips just to remind you how 'to put it in writing':

- Think before you write. If you rush straight into print without thinking about what you want to say, you are liable to ramble. There is nothing like a piece of unconstructed rambling to put the reader off.

- If you are writing something that is particularly important write down a few notes first. These help you to marshal your thoughts and will act as guidelines if at any point you forget what you were going to say.

- Make sure that you have spelt all the words correctly. Remember that you cannot always rely on your computer's spell-checker. It might indicate that there was correct in a situation when you meant their.

- Be consistent with your spelling. For example, if you choose to use the –ise ending in verbs instead of the –ize ending, be sure to use it in all relevant verbs throughout your piece of writing.

- Do not mix up British English spelling and American English spelling or British and American vocabulary in one piece of writing. There are major differences between the two. You need to opt for one and stick to it.

- Make sure that you have inserted the appropriate punctuation. Remember, in particular, to start a sentence with a capital letter and to end it with a full stop, question mark or exclamation mark. Use exclamation marks very sparingly. Remember to put apostrophes in the correct place.

- If you include information that is additional to the main statement of a sentence be sure to separate off the additional text by means of a pair of commas, a pair of brackets or a pair of dashes. Commas are the least intrusive. Use dashes sparingly at all times. It is very tempting to overdo their use and they can seem very intrusive.

- Make sure that you have used the correct word. Some words are so alike in some way that they are easily confused. It is worth checking that you have made the right choice.

- In a formal piece of writing do not use contracted forms such *as don't, isn't, you're* and *he'll.* Use the full forms, as in *do not, is not, you are* and *he will.*

- Avoid using clichés in a formal piece of writing. They have their place in spoken English and in informal written English, but, even there, they should not be overused.

- Avoid using colloquialisms and slang in formal pieces of writing.

- Avoid using jargon unless you happen to be writing to a work colleague or to someone who does the same kind of work as you do, in which case you will both be familiar with the jargon used in your workplace. Do not inflict jargon on others who may not be familiar with the words or their meanings.

- Avoid using words, such as epic and iconic, that are already so over-used that they have become virtually meaningless.

- Do not try to be too clever in your choice of words. For example, the verb use is fine in most contexts and you do not have to seek out such expressions as utilize or put into service. Avoid using difficult words that you might not know the meaning of, especially if you are simply trying to impress. You might well end up sounding pompous rather than impressive.

- Avoid being long-winded. Aim for conciseness and simplicity, especially if the purpose of your piece of writing is to convey information. Your aim should be to make your work as comprehensible and accessible as possible.

- Keep your sentences and paragraphs reasonably short and clear.

- If you are aiming to produce a piece of writing that is more stylish and interesting than something that just conveys information, try adding some variety. Vary the length of your sentences and introduce a range of conjunctions. Do not stick solely to the use of and and but. Do not always begin your sentences with a main clause. Remember that it is acceptable now to have paragraphs of two sentences, or even one, if you are doing this to achieve a particular effect.

- If you choose to use an idiom make sure you have got the wording right. For example, if you want to use the idiom a shot across your bows, which means 'something given as a warning', check that you have not used the word boughs instead of the word bows in error. Because idioms are often used in spoken English it is common not to know how to spell some of their key words. Also make sure you have the meaning correct. Some idioms develop more than one meaning and this can cause confusion. For example, the phrase gunning for someone or something originally meant 'planning to harm someone or something'. Now it can also mean 'very anxious to achieve something', such as a particular job. This meaning is now the more popular and this can cause confusion.

- Avoid redundant words. For example, in the expression a necessary requisite the adjective necessary is redundant as the noun requisite already covers the notion of being necessary. This is also called tautology, i.e. the use of more than one word to convey the same idea.

If you have taken on board the contents of this book, you should now be armed with enough knowledge on the intricacies of English usage to write well and confidently. Good luck!